Identity Safe Classrooms

Places to Belong and Learn

Dorothy M. Steele, EdD

Becki Cohn-Vargas, EdD

Foreword by Linda Darling-Hammond, EdD

CORWIN
A SAGE Company

CORWIN
A SAGE Company

FOR INFORMATION:

Corwin
A SAGE Company
2455 Teller Road
Thousand Oaks, California 91320
(800) 233-9936
www.corwin.com

SAGE Publications Ltd.
1 Oliver's Yard
55 City Road
London, EC1Y 1SP
United Kingdom

SAGE Publications India Pvt. Ltd.
B 1/I 1 Mohan Cooperative Industrial Area
Mathura Road, New Delhi
India 110 044

SAGE Publications Asia-Pacific Pte. Ltd.
3 Church Street
#10-04 Samsung Hub
Singapore 049483

Acquisitions Editor: Dan Alpert
Associate Editor: Kimberly Greenberg
Editorial Assistant: Heidi Arndt
Production Editor: Melanie Birdsall
Copy Editor: Cate Huisman
Typesetter: Hurix Systems Private (P) Ltd.
Proofreader: Theresa Kay
Indexer: David Luljak
Cover Designer: Karine Hovsepian

Some definitions throughout the text were adapted from Steele, D. M. (2012). Identity safe school environment, creating. In J. A. Banks (Ed.), *Encyclopedia of Diversity in Education* (2), 1125–1128. Thousand Oaks, CA: Sage.

Printed in the United States of America

Library of Congress Cataloging-in-Publication Data

Steele, Dorothy M.

Identity safe classrooms : places to belong and learn / Dorothy M. Steele, Becki Cohn-Vargas.

pages cm

Includes bibliographical references and index.

ISBN 978-1-4522-3090-0 (pbk.)

1. Educational sociology. 2. Classroom environment. 3. Multicultural education. I. Cohn-Vargas, Becki. II. Title.

LC191.4.S735 2013

306.43—dc23

2013014824

This book is printed on acid-free paper.

13 14 15 16 17 10 9 8 7 6 5 4 3 2 1

Identity Safe
Classrooms

Contents

Download PDF versions of the
book's tools for reflection at
www.corwin.com/identitysafe.
Access additional materials and information at
identitysafeclassrooms.org.

Foreword

This book offers a rare gift: Drawing on an extraordinary base of both practice and research, it paints a vivid picture of how to create intellectually exciting and psychologically supportive classrooms that enable children to succeed. Rather than pursuing the false quest for a single silver bullet, Dorothy Steele and Becki Cohn-Vargas acknowledge and unpack the multiple dimensions of teaching for social, emotional, and cognitive development. They provide a *whole child, whole classroom* picture of instruction that illustrates how inclusive, academically engaging, and socially aware classrooms promote learning among all students.

This well-painted picture—based on carefully assembled evidence—provides a map for teachers and school leaders, and for educators of these professionals, about how to develop an integrated and coherent approach to instruction that helps students develop academically, socially, emotionally, and ethically. Many aspects of this approach have been described elsewhere in the literature as progressive, child-centered, or culturally responsive. This book brings a careful empirical lens to defining, measuring, and describing the elements of curriculum and teaching that support development and learning while bringing a teacher voice to the description of what educators do day-by-day to create engaging classrooms where children thrive in every way.

A key concept in this book is the notion of *identity safety.* Much more than a feel-good effort to boost students' self-esteem, this idea includes the range of classroom practices that offer cognitively meaningful learning opportunities along with the supports to take full advantage of them. Key parts of this configuration of practices are those that enable students to feel that their social identity is an asset, that they are valuable and welcomed members of the classroom, and that they have a range of peer and teacher supports that will help them succeed. Research finds that these practices positively influence student learning and attachment to school, even in the face of powerful social inequalities students may confront. This book is distinguished by its ability to bring leading-edge psychological research out of the lab and into the classroom in a way that can be understood and used by educators.

The many examples throughout this rich account show how a foundation for growth is built on acknowledging and appreciating what each child brings to school—his or her experiences, interests, culture, language, family roots, talents, and distinct ways of being and knowing in the world. It illustrates how students and teachers succeed together when these starting points are treated as sources for intellectual growth and guidance and when different approaches to communicating and learning are incorporated into classroom life.

In giving voice to teachers who have created classrooms built on positive relationships, trust, and challenging curriculum, this book also offers an antidote to the persistent teacher bashing that has characterized recent "reform" initiatives in the United States. It puts the teachers' role in creating child-centered classrooms front and center, and it celebrates the role of teachers in creating classrooms that promote learning and development for all children.

The practices brought to life in this book can allow us to develop schools as places that empower all students to own their own learning, to become efficacious in pursuing their own goals by helping others to participate in building a healthier and more just society. In such schools, all students will experience high expectations and encounter academic work that calls for critical thinking and problem solving around real world concerns that provoke passion and commitment to learning. In such schools, students will have multiple ways to demonstrate their learning through authentic assessments. In such schools, students' capacity to succeed and excel will be built on trusting relationships between and among students and staff that extend to families and communities as well.

The research presented here reveals that schools engaging in these practices produce stronger learning in many ways, including on standardized tests. However, that is not the most important aspect of this work. In a society where high-quality education has too often been confused with meeting test score targets, we need portraits of the kinds of educational settings where students can experience affirmation, joy, discovery, and meaning. We need images of how the families, cultures, and experiences of students can be integrated into the tapestry of the classroom. And we need depictions of how students flourish in such environments. This book provides all of that and more. It is a gift from which educators and children will benefit in as many ways as the multifaceted elements of learning and teaching are illuminated in these pages.

—*Linda Darling-Hammond*
Stanford University
April 21, 2013

Acknowledgments

DOROTHY STEELE'S ACKNOWLEDGMENTS

My life has been rich in opportunities to work with many generous people who have taught me everything I have learned about how children learn and what teachers need in order to help them. I will try here to do their immeasurable contributions justice.

The work on identity safety described in this book has a long history, beginning in 1998 when a small group of us began to meet to explore whether and how teachers could create classrooms in which students of color could become more successful by being freed from the threat of being negatively stereotyped in school. Without this research group's strong dedication to this question and expertise in designing a large, school-based study to answer our questions, this work would not have succeeded.

This group consisted of Claude Steele, whose original work on stereotype threat provides the foundation of identity safety; Hazel Rose Markus, a Stanford University social psychologist whose work has focused on the powerful influence of culture on experience and behavior; Michael Kass, an educator who has been a kindergarten teacher, principal, and activist devoted to equity in schools; the late Dan Solomon, another social psychologist who served as the director of research at the Child Development Project in Oakland, whose expertise on observational data helped us develop and analyze our research tools; and finally, Francie Green, the research coordinator who helped us plan for the many considerations and carry out all the needed tasks to conduct a year-long research project in multiple schools.

Generous grants from the Russell Sage Foundation funded this research and supported the group of teachers who met with us monthly for over two years following the data collection to think about how to incorporate our findings into daily practice. Much gratitude goes to Eric Wanner, president of the foundation, who generously supported our work.

It is humbling to consider the numbers of people on whom we depended to carry out this research. They include the 84 teachers who allowed us into their classrooms many times in one year, the six classroom observers who carefully collected and documented the data throughout the year, the principals of the 13 schools, and the superintendent and her cabinet who accepted our work into their midst. Importantly, the school secretaries, who worked with our research coordinator to match complex school schedules to orchestrate all these visits, deserve our deep gratitude.

Many people gave freely of their time to think about how to analyze the vast amount of data and interpret it so that teachers could benefit from what we learned. These include dear friends, Paul Davies, who was then Claude Steele's postdoctoral student and is now a professor of psychology at the University of British Columbia at Okanagan; and Tyrone Forman and Amanda Lewis, who were then visiting fellows at Stanford's Center for Comparative Studies in Race and Ethnicity and who are now both professors of sociology at Emory University. They worked with the research team, Claude, Hazel, Dan, Francie, and me to help us get a handle on all the data.

I thank also Leanne Isaak who, with lots of grace and competence, worked to keep me on track in my role as executive director at the Center for Comparative Studies in Race and Ethnicity during the years we were busy with the research project; Milton Reynolds, who was one of our classroom observers and now serves as a teacher educator with the organization Facing History; and Adi Lapin, a professional developer and program manager of Beginning Teacher Support and Assessment (BTSA) in our research district who, with Milton, has continued to work with the new teachers in that district to help them incorporate identity safe teaching practices into their classrooms. I continue to learn from them about this process, which is inspired by their deep dedication to making school a better place for all children and their teachers. Their commitment has encouraged me to keep my focus on finishing the book and sharing it with teachers.

Becki Cohn-Vargas, my coauthor, is totally responsible for turning this work into a book. She pushed this idea when I couldn't really listen, and kept talking about it, unfazed by my resistant behavior. She found our wonderful editor, Dan Alpert, who made the idea seem real. Meeting Dan was the clincher. I knew we could make this happen. Becki's commitment to true equity in schools is matched only by her broad intellect. Her ability to connect experience to theory and back again makes working with her profoundly engaging, and it moved us toward this shared goal of encouraging teachers in this most important profession. Becki is a great friend whose thoughtfulness and generous spirit have sustained our work over these last few years.

Other friends helped me keep on track in direct and indirect ways. I want to especially thank four people who read our book and gave comments that improved it. They are Doug Foster, professor of journalism; Jay Rosner, lawyer and advocate for students; Adi Lapin, educator; and Amanda Lewis, sociology professor. Their varied backgrounds helped us to look at our writing from different perspectives. Their enduring friendship means more than I can say.

Finally, I return to two members of the original research team, Hazel Rose Markus and Claude Steele. Hazel has been Claude's colleague for more than 25 years and our dear friend for that time as well. It was her willingness to participate in this research that brought me into the circle of researchers and gave my developing ideas voice. For that, I cannot thank her enough. Her friendship sustains me in work and family life.

From the moment I met Claude nearly 50 years ago, my life opened to ideas and experiences I could not have dreamed of. His persistent interest in "how life works," how to make things better, how to include those who have not yet been included, and how to constantly try to develop one's intellect shapes our lives every day. These passions are embodied in a person who is loving, kind, and full of humor.

Together we have made a happy life woven together by our work and love of our family. Our children, Jory and Benny, and their spouses, Sidney and Dayna, give us roots to the earth that help make me strong every day. Their children, Matthew and Coleman, remind me what my parents taught me by example, to treat every child as a gift to be cherished.

BECKI COHN-VARGAS'S ACKNOWLEDGMENTS

I come from a family of teachers and would like to acknowledge their deep influence on me: my grandmother Elsa Rhee, who taught in Germany before the Holocaust, when she was forced to flee; my mother Eva Cohn, who was a revered teacher for 30 years in Palo Alto, California; my father Cantor Hans Cohn, who taught hundreds of bar mitzvah students, among others; and my stepmother Nina Loban, who teaches piano. Along with love and support, they have been models for me and have instilled a spirit of service and a belief in education as the hope for the future. They also instilled in me a belief in human capacity and a passion for equity and social justice.

I want to thank my husband and children, who have been alongside me in this journey. I met Rito Vargas 31 years ago in Nicaragua, where we worked together filming preschool children. (He filmed, and I was the producer.) Our three children, Priscilla Vargas, Melania Vargas, and David Vargas, have been my greatest teachers as I traveled the path of parenting. Now they are my sounding boards, my proofreaders, and my cheering squad.

Other family members have also been instrumental and nurtured me along the way, including my two sisters and their families: Ruth Cohn and her husband Michael Lewin, and Barbara Liepman and her husband Michael Liepman, as well as their children Ben and Allison and my niece Julia Rhee, who I now mentor as she teaches in the inner city of Richmond, California. I also want to acknowledge my husband's family, particularly Felipa Cintron, Ethel Martinez, Maria de los Angeles Montcrieffe, Elizabeth Montcrieffe, and Marta Ibarra.

I particularly want to highlight two educators who guided me along the path and deeply embraced identity safety: Joyce Germaine-Watts, my doctoral advisor, and my dear friend Kathe Gogolewski, who I met as my daughter's most amazing third grade teacher and who has worked side by side with me on all equity and writing projects for the last 20 years. Other close friends have also supported me: Reverend Robin Mathews-Johnson, Randi Thomson, Patrice O'Neill, Martha Booz, and Laurie Bernstein.

This book includes the voices of many teachers and administrators. I particularly want to thank Max Velez, Mangla Oza, Katie Bimpson, Arlinda Smith, Jennifer Abrams, Letitia Burton, Danae Reynolds, Meg Williams, Cathy Howard, Keith Libert, K. J. Lee, Laura Joy Lamkin, Jen Corn, and Marilyn Cook, educators from Oakland, Palo Alto, Berkeley, and San Jose, California, for their wisdom and deep exploration of identity safety. They are really just a small part of the hundreds of dedicated educators we have met over the years who truly care for their students and cultivate those students' identities like precious shoots and roots. The amazing students of all ages we have known and continue to know are our inspiration, and for them we have done this work.

Finally, I want to thank my coauthor Dorothy Steele for her inspiration. She has influenced my life for the last 18 years, starting when we worked together as professional developers at the Developmental Studies Center. She even advised me on how to help my young daughter with her attitude about being a mixed-race child. I still remember the day I ran into her in a classroom where she was beginning observations for identity safety, and she told me what she was doing. This work immediately resonated with me, and I brought it into my district and eventually my dissertation. Dorothy and I have had a wonderful time writing this book, grappling with ideas, drawing from the best moments of our practice, and sharing our lives along this journey.

Together, we want to thank Dan Alpert and Heidi Arndt of Corwin. Dan has been an awesome editor who truly believes in this work and has offered untold support. We also want to thank all the readers and reviewers who helped along the way.

PUBLISHER'S ACKNOWLEDGMENTS

Corwin gratefully acknowledges the contributions of the following reviewers:

Susan Adkins
Teacher
Detroit Public Schools
Detroit, MI

Roxie R. Ahlbrecht
Math Recovery Intervention Specialist
Lowell MST Elementary School
Sioux Falls, SD

Susan Schipper
Teacher
Charles Street School
Palmyra, NJ

About the Authors

Dorothy M. Steele, EdD, is the former executive director of the Center for Comparative Studies in Race and Ethnicity at Stanford University. She is an early childhood educator who is interested in teaching in public schools, including teaching practices that are effective for diverse classrooms, alternative assessment processes that inform teaching and learning, and strategies that build inclusive communities of learners. Her work with the Stanford Integrated Schools Project (SISP) was an attempt to look at these various aspects of schooling in a large urban school district.

Dorothy began her work with teachers and children in 1968 in Columbus, Ohio, as the director/teacher of one of the city's first Head Start programs. During the 1970s, she served as the curriculum coordinator for the City of Seattle's children's programs, as an early childhood teacher educator, as a parent educator, and, for eight years, as the director of a large, university-based child care center.

In 1987, Dorothy began her doctoral work in early childhood education and, with her advisor, developed an alternative assessment process for early childhood education, the Work Sampling System that is now being used throughout the world. Her dissertation explored the negative impact of standardized tests on kindergarten teachers' educational decisions for their students.

Dorothy received her AB in music from Hiram College in Hiram, Ohio, in 1967; her MA in early childhood education from The Ohio State University in 1971; and her EdD in early childhood education from the University of Michigan in 1994.

She lives in Stanford, California, with her husband, Claude M. Steele. Their family includes a son and daughter and their spouses and two energetic and loving preschool-age boys who make life ever more sweet.

Becki Cohn-Vargas, EdD, is currently the director of Not In Our School, a national nonprofit working group. She designs curriculum, coaches school staff, and produces films and digital media on models for creating safe and inclusive schools, free of bullying and intolerance. She also teaches online courses on bullying prevention for the University of San Diego. Becki worked in educational settings for more than 35 years as a teacher and administrator.

Becki began her career in early childhood education at the West Santa Rosa Multicultural Center in rural Sonoma County, California, in 1975. She did community service in Central America in the Guatemalan Highlands and later in the Preschool Department of the Nicaraguan Ministry of Education. She then returned to California and worked as a bilingual teacher and principal in Oakland, as a curriculum director in Palo Alto, and most recently as superintendent–principal of a one-school district in San Jose. She also worked as a staff developer for the Child Development Program of the Developmental Studies Center. In each of these settings, she focused on developing and implementing effective teaching strategies for diverse student populations and creating environments that promoted educational equity. In 2003, she learned of the research on identity safety with SISP and designed a follow-up study with a group of elementary school teachers. Her doctoral dissertation focused on identifying, describing, and implementing identity safe practices.

Becki received a bachelor's degree and teaching credential from Sonoma State University; a master's in education from California State University, East Bay; and a doctorate from Fielding Graduate University. She and her husband live in El Sobrante, California, and have three adult children living in the Bay Area. With her husband Rito Vargas, Becki is also working to develop an environmental research center on their private reserve in the Nicaraguan rain forest.

Part I

Getting Started

Welcome to Readers

1

The purpose of this book is to engage teachers in thinking about how their everyday practice influences students from diverse backgrounds from a new perspective. Though teachers think about teaching and learning continually, their voices are rarely heard. Instead, the relentless debate in the news media about how to improve American schools and reduce the achievement gap focuses on a blame game that points to teachers or parents or students as the cause of what is too often described as the "failure" of American schools. Teachers are vilified as lazy, incompetent, and ruled by union decisions. Parents are blamed for raising unruly, disrespectful children. And students' capabilities and motivations are questioned. Recommendations for improving schools include ridding districts of teachers unions, replacing regular public schools with charter schools, and using punitive discipline methods such as zero tolerance policies as punishment for unwanted student behavior. Much of the discourse is about student performance rather than student learning. As a nation, we have nearly lost the plot of the purpose of education. The idea that a good education could teach students to become productive contributors to our democratic society is rarely mentioned.

Few of the discussions about school improvement focus on what is going on in the classroom and how that affects the students' daily experience. And, not many of the media reports and talk show discussions on "the gap" describe how students are treated or how to build their skills, challenge their curiosity, or help them learn to work together and independently on meaningful, useful learning activities. This is particularly true when the focus is on schools that students of color and poor students attend. For these students, the recommendations focus on strict discipline, remedial curriculum aimed at teaching basic skills, and almost military-like requirements for compliant behavior. These remedies are celebrated as successful models for other schools to follow. The media discourse is focused on solutions such as these for low-performing schools attended by other people's children. Few promote the idea that we should treat all students as we would want our own children treated. And, it is rarely recommended that we treat teachers with the respect and authority needed for them to build intellectually and socially dynamic, caring classrooms focused on learning. Yet, mutual respect among all members of the classroom community provides the foundation for creating what we call an *identity safe classroom.*

Our premise is that efforts to create identity safe classrooms are essential to protect the lives of all students, especially those who suffer from two conditions: (1) a sense of alienation from school after repeated failure and (2) the epidemic of punitive punishments including suspensions and expulsions. These punitive discipline practices are *not* colorblind. A national study of nearly 7,000 districts in 2009–2010 found that 17.7% of African American students and 7.5% of Latino students were suspended from school during the school year. These high numbers are in contrast to those for Asian students (2.1%) and white students (5.6%). This disparity in suspension rates is called *disproportionality* and leads to the "school-to-prison pipeline" that describes the troubling trajectory of young students of color when their abilities at school are negatively stereotyped (Losen & Gillespie, 2012). It is important to make clear that the majority of these decisions to exclude students from school are based on discretionary disciplinary actions in response to behaviors such as acting disrespectful or defiant; they are not based on more serious offenses such as fighting or possessing drugs (Drakeford, 2006).

In response to the unintended consequences of these disciplinary practices, some schools have to begun to examine them and seek solutions other than exclusion from school, which has been found to have a negative affect on students instead of helping them improve their behavior. As teachers look at data on achievement and behavior, they see the links between academic failure, alienation from school, and disruptive behavior and can seek solutions that address all aspects of a child's school experience. Our work on identity safety focuses on all aspects of life in the classroom and helps teachers examine their practice from the point of view of each of their students. This process helps them respond more successfully to the needs of each member of their class.

INTRODUCTION OF IDENTITY SAFE TEACHING PRACTICES

Our work is based on the premise that classrooms are socially dynamic places where, for each student, who you are and what matters to you is inextricably linked to your sense of belonging and ability to fully engage in learning and participating.

Our research identified an array of effective practices that are linked to improved student outcomes on standardized tests and on students' attitudes about school, including their overall liking for school, educational aspirations, and sense of belonging in school.

In our yearlong research on 84 diverse elementary classrooms, we have documented ways that teachers can create inclusive, intellectually exciting, and socially supportive classrooms that promote learning and social development among all students. This research, funded by the Russell Sage Foundation and called the Stanford Integrated Schools Project (SISP), identified certain characteristics of the classroom that had a positive effect on student learning and attachment to schooling, in spite of real and powerful social inequalities in these schools. These identified classroom practices and relationships foster a sense of *identity safety* in students. Students have a sense of identity safety when they believe that their social identity is an asset, rather than a barrier to success in the classroom, and that they are welcomed, supported, and valued whatever their background.

Identity safe practices provide a potential antidote to a sense of *stereotype threat* that has been shown to lower academic achievement. Stereotype threat theory suggests that people from groups whose abilities in school are negatively stereotyped may worry that they could "be judged or treated in terms of the stereotype or that [they] might do something that would inadvertently confirm it" (Steele, C. M., Spencer, & Aronson, 2002, p. 389). The research on stereotype threat and its link to depressed performance in important domains of human learning and performance provides the theoretical foundation of the present work on identity safety for students.

To answer our question, "What can teachers do in diverse classrooms to promote more successful learning and attachment to school," SISP researchers observed 84 classrooms three times during this yearlong study to identify classroom practices that teachers can incorporate to promote learning among those students whose ability and behavior at school is commonly questioned. The researchers observed everything in the classrooms to see what teachers can do to create a classroom environment that serves as an antidote to the threat of being stereotyped as a poor student. As we will show, this antidote, *identity safe teaching practices,* benefits everyone in the classroom. All students make progress when teachers focus on positive classroom relationships, challenging learning opportunities, and cooperation instead of competition, to build on all students' knowledge, curiosity, and energy.

Identity safe teaching is not colorblind. Instead, it uses student diversity as a resource for learning. Identity safe classrooms are free from the negative relationships, cues, and teaching practices (e.g., tracking, punitive discipline, remedial curriculum) that implicitly or explicitly link students' identities (e.g., race, gender, class) to academic performance. Identity safe teaching practices begin with the consideration of how every aspect of classroom life is being experienced by each of the students in the class. We discovered that with careful attention to providing challenging instruction and by facilitating positive social dynamics in the classroom, students of all backgrounds come to feel accepted, included, and expected to be successful. They can begin to feel identity safe!

RESEARCH BASIS OF IDENTITY SAFETY

The goal of racially integrating schools, the aim of the 1954 *Brown v. Board of Education* decision, was expected to fix the problem of unequal schooling for minority students. But now, as our schools become ever more segregated once again, we realize that access to equal schooling is just the start of the endeavor to provide America's students of color with adequate schooling that promotes success in school and later adult life. Once students have access to the same classrooms, the complicated work begins—how to make classrooms a place of inclusion and high-level learning for all students.

As mentioned earlier, the work on identity safety emerged out of the research on stereotype threat. Our question was, if stereotype threat depresses performance, is there anything that teachers can do to create a less threatening environment to free students to learn? Based on earlier research and theorizing (Davies, Spencer, & Steele, C. M., 2005; Markus, Steele, C. M., & Steele, D. M., 2000; Steele, C. M., & Aronson, 1995; Steele, C. M., Spencer, & Aronson, 2002), we began with the assumption that particular practices (e.g., ability tracking, colorblind approaches to curriculum materials and tasks, rigid teaching strategies) in integrated classrooms may, inadvertently, reinforce widely held negative stereotypes linking ethnicity to academic achievement and leading to reduced achievement for students of color. Our SISP study was designed to test whether other practices (e.g., a focus on cooperative, helpful student relationships, expressed and scaffolded high expectations for all students, challenging curriculum) would cultivate a sense of identity safety in students (a sense of freedom from stereotypes linking social identity to academic performance) and would improve the academic achievement of many minority students.

We know from the experimental work on stereotype threat among college students that performance can be improved by explicitly removing stereotype threat from the situation (Cohen, Steele, C. M., & Ross, 1999;

Davies, Spencer, & Steele, C. M., 2005; Steele, C. M., & Aronson, 1995). This work shows that there are various ways of reducing these forms of identity threat: promoting cross-group friendships, fostering high expectations for success, providing success-affirming role models, eliciting and valuing diverse perspectives and ideas, and providing an array of diverse representations linking people from diverse groups with valued classroom membership and academic achievement. While some teachers are using several of these practices, we recognized that sustaining them in the classroom day in and day out over the school year would be crucial to diminish the effects of stereotype threat. We hypothesized that when some constellation of these practices is intentionally incorporated in a classroom setting, all students, and particularly students of color, will be more successful than they would be in less identity safe classrooms.

Our work on identity safe teaching practices was an effort to translate the findings of the research on college students into elementary classrooms. There is ethnographic data indicating that young students are aware when some students but not others are disproportionately being sent to the principal's office, when some students but not others are in the high reading group, when some parents but not others are invited to help with a field trip, and so forth (Ambady, Shih, Kim, & Pitinsky, 2001; Lewis, 2004). We believe that it is practices such as these that contribute to students' learning about negative stereotypes.

By contrast, we found in our SISP research that a set of factors, taken together, can mitigate the identity threat that prevails in many integrated classrooms. These practices we call identity safe teaching practices can create a social and intellectual environment of inclusion and validation that can be experienced even by young children.

These four domains that constitute identity safe teaching practices are the following:

1. *Child-Centered Teaching* characterized by Classroom Autonomy, Listening for Students' Voices, Teaching for Understanding, and a Focus on Cooperation

2. *Cultivating Diversity as a Resource*, characterized by Diversity as a Resource for Teaching, Challenging Curriculum, and High Expectations and Academic Rigor

3. *Classroom Relationships* characterized by Teacher Warmth, Teacher Availability to Support Learning, and Positive Student Relationships

4. *Caring Environments* characterized by Emotional and Physical Comfort, which is promoted by Teacher Skill and Attention to Prosocial Development

These four domains reflect the foundational assumption of identity safety that learning is a social process. Learning occurs in every social, intellectual, and procedural transaction between the teacher and students and among the students. Therefore, it is important to foster positive, caring relationships with the other students and the teacher in the classroom. Because relationships matter, who you are and what you know and can do matters. While a teacher may have the idea that being colorblind and ignoring differences shows equal acceptance of all, even young students are very aware of their differences. Instead, in identity safe environments, student differences are recognized and validated. Consideration is given to every aspect of the classroom, to all the subtle and overt messages that recognize that diverse ideas, perspectives, and materials can actually enhance learning.

WHAT'S WRONG WITH BEING COLORBLIND?

Part of what makes it difficult for teachers to fully appreciate group differences in lived experience and their role in academic achievement is the well-intended cultural injunction *not to see* group differences. Since the civil rights era, the social norm has been to remedy the negative effects of historic group prejudice by not seeing group differences. The goal, then, has been to be colorblind. It is linked to our idea of fairness and the strongly held belief that, in America, if you work hard you can achieve anything. This belief is based on the notion that people are equal, so that race and ethnicity should not affect opportunities in life such as education, housing, and employment. Yet, in reality, people are not colorblind and, from a young age, children in this country are exposed to the powerful influence of race. And such efforts not to see differences can often magnify the impact of differences (Markus, Steele, C. M., & Steele, D. M., 2000).

It is important to note here that the theory of stereotype threat is not based on the assumption that teachers are personally or explicitly prejudiced. Quite the contrary, we believe that the goal of most teachers is to be fair by being colorblind. However, this well-meaning goal to ignore differences inadvertently creates an environment that can lead to stereotype threat among students. By not paying *particular* attention to who each student is and by failing to address each student's *particular* experiences and interests, teachers unintentionally convey that what these students know and can do, and how they feel, does not matter. Without cues in the environment that reflect the lives, interests, and value of these students, they become, in the term of Ralph Ellison (1952), invisible.

FROM THEORY, TO RESEARCH, TO TRANSFORMING PRACTICE

Many of the numerous explanations for the persistent gap in achievement between white children and children of color focus on attributes of the children and their families as the source of the problem. This perspective about the source of the gap has been dominant since our earliest attempts at school integration. There have been alternative perspectives, though, that shift the focus from the troubled characteristics of the students to the experience they have in schools. As long ago as 1933, historian Carter G. Woodson wrote in his book *The Mis-Education of the Negro,*

> The so-called modern education, with all its defects, however, does others so much more good than it does the Negro, because it has been worked out in conformity to the needs of those who have enslaved and oppressed weaker people. . . . No systemic effort towards change has been possible for, taught the same economics, history, philosophy, literature and religion which have established the present code of morals, the Negro's mind has been brought under the control of his oppressor. The problem of holding the Negro down, therefore, is easily solved. When you control a man's thinking you do not have to worry about his actions. (1933, pp. xii–xiii)

If the problem of the achievement gap rests in students' fixed ability and motivation, there is no reason for schools to change their approach to teaching—the problem *is* with the children. Inherent in school improvement efforts is the assumption that schools *can* do something to improve student learning, in spite of the structural and familial situations from which students come. The comprehensive, national school improvement efforts of James Comer (1988), Henry Levin (1988), and the Child Development Project (Solomon, Watson, Battistich, Schaps, & Delucchi, 1996) all point to the power that teachers and schools have to improve student learning, thereby changing students' schooling outcomes. In addition to demonstrating the effect that teaching practices can have on improving student learning, these three research programs informed the process of building our hypotheses about what might constitute identity safe teaching practices and might be linked to improvement in students' sense of being identity safe. Our hypothesis was that freeing students from distracting threats to their identity in these ways should foster their higher academic achievement, sense of belonging, and social understanding.

Following our year-long observation of 84 elementary classrooms, the SISP team met for over two years with teachers and administrators from the research district to take the findings of the study back to them and to form a community of inquiry about how to implement the identity safe practices identified in the study. Much was learned from the teachers in this monthly study group as they grappled together with how to incorporate these practices in the daily life of the classroom. For example, teachers considered how to move from competition to cooperation, how to truly offer all students appropriately challenging curriculum, and how to find time to focus on prosocial development.

A few years later, a second research initiative brought together a small group of teachers who held a monthly study group for a year that focused on exploring each of the identity safe factors. These teachers' efforts to understand and to begin to incorporate identity safe practices were documented in Becki's dissertation (2007). Some real-life examples from her dissertation, drawn from the inquiry and practice of teachers in the two study groups, are included in this book, and we hope that they will inspire and inform readers.

IDENTITY SAFETY BRINGS TOGETHER BEST PRACTICES

As we shared what we learned from the SISP study with teachers in many different settings, we found that the theory and practices of identity safety resonate with educators as they face the complexity of creating environments that promote teaching and learning of students from a range of backgrounds.

Teachers who are educating students to navigate the complexities of the 21st century are seeking to make their classrooms places that foster creativity, critical thinking, a sense of responsibility toward others, and a strong foundation in literacy and numeracy. They are aware that their students need social-emotional learning, prosocial skills, and tools for cooperating, communicating, and fostering empathy. As classrooms are increasingly diverse, many schools are seeking culturally responsive ways to help students learn to appreciate their identities and strengths, bridge differences, and understand multiple perspectives. Identity safe teaching incorporates each of these critical areas of the process of teaching and learning.

Identity safe teaching practices fit well with the Common Core State Standards. These standards encourage teaching for understanding and promote performance-based assessments rather than just rote learning measured on multiple-choice tests. Identity safety is amenable to project-based learning that seeks to get children thinking autonomously and using their learning in new and innovative situations. Teachers are also seeking to meaningfully differentiate their instruction and to provide explicit teaching and behavioral support for each of their students.

Many identity safe practices will be familiar to veteran teachers. For example, cooperative learning is a practice that has been around for many years and lends itself to a more equitable classroom where students feel more identity safe. Some experienced teachers might even say, "Isn't this just good teaching?" However, we contend that identity safety, while encompassing the practices that are good for all children, has been demonstrated to improve learning for students of color. We ask readers to take a deeper look at how these practices that focus on each student's social identity will transform student learning outcomes.

It is our hope that this book will help teachers do two things. First, we hope they will look at life in the classroom every day from the perspective of each of the students and make modifications that support students' sense of identity safety. Second, we hope teachers will build on what they know and do and become intentional in using the time-tested, equitable practices and new ideas described in this book to create classrooms that are more identity safe. When teachers do this, their students will become more successful, both academically and socially.

How to Use This Book

2

Our intention in writing this book is to bring the research and findings of the Stanford Integrated Schools Project (SISP) on identity safety to educators in a way that they can immediately begin to put into practice. Included are the voices of the teachers who participated in a case study as they began to implement identity safe practices into their classrooms. Their efforts are documented in Becki's dissertation on identity safety (Cohn-Vargas, 2007). It is our hope that preservice, beginning, and veteran teachers, administrators, and others can use the book in any manner that supports their efforts to consider their classrooms from the perspectives of the various students whom they teach. As they reflect on life in their classrooms from many perspectives, we hope this book will support their engagement with questions, big and little, about the purpose of education, the goals they have for students, and how what they do every day moves students toward these goals, or not. We might even say that our hope is that, by engaging in these questions, they will be free to see their students with "new eyes" and see in them higher possibilities for their success in school and in later life. And, finally, we hope that teachers and other educators who are often represented so negatively will appreciate, once again, the importance of what they do every day. We hope that those who read and talk about this book will feel honored and more identity safe themselves.

To engage in this process, educators may read this book from start to finish or choose any chapter that addresses their present interest as the starting point. It might be read in a study group or alone. Readers will see that many ideas appear in more than one chapter, because each aspect of identity safety is related to the others. For example, one cannot have a classroom focused on challenging curriculum for some students but not others and achieve any sense that the teacher holds high expectations for each student's academic success. Or, one cannot focus on cooperation instead of competition without teaching students how to work together in a positive and productive manner. In describing the ideas of identity safe throughout the book, we look at the process of creating an identity safe classroom as a whole, but we also break the concept down into its component pieces so that teachers can get a handle on each element of identity safety. In every element of identity safety described throughout the book, the focus is on how teachers in diverse classrooms can use the resources brought by all students and respond to their needs in many different ways. Additional information and activities can be found at **identitysafeclassrooms.org**.

HOW THE BOOK IS ORGANIZED

The core of our book is written in four parts. They describe the four domains that make up identity safe teaching: *Child-Centered Teaching, Cultivating Diversity as a Resource, Classroom Relationships,* and *Caring Classrooms.* Each of these four domains is composed of three or four chapters that describe in detail one of the factors of identity safety found in the SISP study.

The chapters are all organized in the same manner. Every chapter begins with a complete definition of the factor and the reason it is important to the process. Each contains ideas from teachers and the authors about *how* to incorporate these practices into daily life in the classroom. For example, the chapter on prosocial development includes practices that can help teachers promote social development: class meetings, cooperative learning, and integrating prosocial learning into academic lessons.

Every chapter includes Challenges and Dilemmas. Our purpose in presenting these challenges and dilemmas is to identify particular areas in each of these factors that educators must grapple with when incorporating these ideas into their classrooms. We close each chapter with one or two activities to engage teachers in applying the practices, either individually or in study groups.

The teachers you will hear from throughout this book are the authors' colleagues and the authors themselves. Most prominent are the teachers who were involved in the study groups, including the many teachers from the research district who initiated this process and the four teachers who provided a case study of the process of implementing identity safety into their classrooms. Other teacher colleagues represented in the book are from various districts and are people with whom the authors have worked in different capacities. They teach in elementary classrooms with students from diverse backgrounds who represent a range of socioeconomic levels. From these many teachers and children, the authors have learned almost everything they know, and it is their goal to share this with you, the reader.

Part I References

Ambady, N., Shih, M., Kim, A., & Pitinsky, T. (2001). Stereotype susceptibility in children: Effects of identity activation on quantitative performance. *Psychological Science, 12*(5), 385–390.

Cohen, G. L., Steele, C. M., & Ross, L. D. (1999). The mentor's dilemma: Providing critical feedback across the racial divide. *Personality & Social Psychology Bulletin, 25,* 1302–1318.

Cohn-Vargas, B. (2007). *Nurturing identity safety in elementary classrooms: A participatory action research study of effective strategies that validate students' backgrounds and cultures while promoting academic and social success* [dissertation]. Fielding Graduate University, Santa Barbara, CA. Available at http://books.google.com/books/about/Nurturing_Identity_Safety_in_Elementary.html?id=1nBqREHiOWYC

Comer, J. P. (1988). Educating poor minority children. *Scientific American, 259*(5), 42–48.

Davies, P. G., Spencer, S., & Steele, C. M. (2005). Clearing the air: Identity safety moderates the effects of stereotype threat on women's leadership aspirations. *Journal of Personality and Social Psychology, 88*(2), 276–287.

Drakeford, W. (2006). *Racial disproportionality in school disciplinary practices.* Retrieved from http://www.nccrest.org/Briefs/School_Discipline_Brief.pdf

Ellison, R. (1952). *Invisible man.* New York, NY: Random House.

Levin, H. (1988). Accelerated schools for disadvantaged students. *Educational Leadership, 44*(6), 19–21.

Lewis, A. E. (2003). *Race in the schoolyard: Negotiating the color line in classrooms and communities.* New Brunswick, NJ: Rutgers University Press.

Losen, D. J., & Gillespie, J. (2012). *Opportunities suspended: The disparate impact of disciplinary exclusion from school.* Los Angeles: The Civil Rights Project. University of California at Los Angeles.

Markus, H. R., Steele, C. M., & Steele, D. M. (2000). The end of tolerance: Engaging cultural differences. *Daedalus, 129*(4), 233–259.

Solomon, D., Watson, M., Battistich, V., Schaps, E., & Delucchi, K. (1996). Creating classrooms that students experience as communities. *American Journal of Community Psychology, 24,* 719–874.

Steele, C. M., & Aronson, J. (1995). Stereotype threat and the intellectual test performance of African Americans. *Journal of Personality and Social Psychology, 69,* 797–811.

Steele, C. M., Spencer, S., & Aronson, J. (2002). Contending with group image: The psychology of stereotype and social identity threat. *Advances in Experimental Social Psychology, 34,* 379–440.

Woodson, C. G. (1933). *The mis-education of the Negro.* Washington, DC: Associated Publishers.

Part II

Child-Centered Teaching

WHAT DO WE MEAN BY CHILD-CENTERED TEACHING?

Child-centered teaching is the practice of putting the students' perspectives at the center of everything that happens in a classroom. One teacher took a few minutes at the end of each day to sit in one of the seats in her classroom. She wanted to look around the room and imagine just what it felt like for that student to be in her classroom. What did the child see when she looked around the class? Did that child see her work on the wall? Did the child see any pictures of other kids who looked like her? What did the child hear when the teacher was speaking? Did she understand what the teacher was saying? Each day, the teacher sat in a different seat to get to know each of her students better.

Child-centered teaching practices "are essential in diverse classrooms to teach students that who you are and what you think are important to the learning process" (Steele, D. M., 2012, p. 1126). These factors of child-centered teaching, taken together, work as strategies teachers can intentionally use to foster a sense of belonging and identification with learning: Listening for Students' Voices, Teaching for Understanding, Focusing on Cooperation (instead of competition among students), and fostering Classroom Autonomy. Here are short definitions of the four factors of child-centered teaching.

Listening for Students' Voices is the foundation of child-centered teaching in identity safe classrooms. When teachers encourage students to participate in the life of the classroom by contributing their thoughts and discussing their interests, students gain a sense of belonging and purpose in school that they cannot get if the teacher makes all the decisions. Teachers can ask students to present and support their ideas and opinions, listen to others and build on their ideas, and help plan activities. Students may even get a rule changed if things are unfair. These opportunities permit students to draw from their own backgrounds, knowledge, curiosity, and energy to contribute to the social and academic learning in the classroom.

Teaching for Understanding rather than teaching focused on learning facts requires a set of strategies that involves student questioning, use of imagination, and elaboration of their own and others' ideas. Lessons can be designed to help students build new understandings; to give students multiple ways to approach tasks, analyze concepts, and apply them in new situations; and to help students to think in a "meta" way about what they are going to study. When students do not understand basic concepts or vocabulary, they become distracted with trying to make sense of what is happening and cannot focus on building new understandings. When teachers observe students regularly, they can determine whether students truly understand the concepts being taught. Teachers will then be able to provide specific feedback to correct any errors.

Focusing on Cooperation happens as teachers structure regular time for students to work on learning tasks that are free of competition and are focused on students collaborating in meaningful ways (Steele, D. M., 2012). Learning to cooperate might be the most important set of skills for students to learn. These skills can immediately serve them during recess and on the street. Practice in cooperating can help students answer questions such as, "Can I take turns on bikes without fighting? Can I solve a problem on the soccer field without it turning into a brawl? Can I speak up when someone is picking on or bullying me or one of my classmates?" Later in life, these cooperation skills mean that students have the ability to work as a team to improve a school, solve a problem in a work setting, or in our case, write this book together.

Supporting Classroom Autonomy means giving students choices in their learning activities and in how they approach these tasks. When students make choices such as which topics to write about, books to read, and activities to participate in, they come to feel that the classroom belongs to everyone in it. In addition, in autonomous classrooms, students do not need to depend solely on the teacher to find answers to questions and can access information and materials as needed.

Taken as a whole, the hoped-for outcomes of child-centered teaching lead to helping students become independent and confident learners who are self-aware and able to work well with others.

In the next four chapters, we will explain why each of the identity safety factors of child-centered teaching is important, and we will give examples of how to put them in practice. We recognize that there will be aspects of each that are hard to implement, so we will highlight some of the challenges and dilemmas and also how these can be addressed.

Throughout the book, we will ask you to examine your own approach to teaching and to reflect on your own social identity as a child and now as an adult. While our focus is on specific classroom strategies that put student experience in the center of classroom life, unless we question our own assumptions we may inadvertently attribute student behaviors to our unexamined notions based on our own experiences and social identities.

Listening for Students' Voices   3

WHY FOCUS ON LISTENING FOR STUDENTS' VOICES?

When students' voices are included in the classroom, students discover their own unique identities and manners of self-expression as well as the confidence to share their thoughts and ideas. Students build confidence when they are given opportunities to express their "voice" through sharing their thoughts and feelings, playing important roles in decision making, and reflecting on their own work and life in the classroom.

One important way for teachers to listen for students' voices is to have students spend time on tasks involving their own ideas, opinions, or experiences. Students can be taught explicitly how and when to state opinions. They can learn how to formulate ideas, give reasons for their points of view, and elaborate on the ideas of others. Students do this by having a say in classroom decisions and by helping to make academic and social choices. These opportunities result in students learning how to express their own opinions, listen to one another, and feel the importance of their participation.

Children have more choices than ever, no matter what socioeconomic level they are from. Through the media and the Internet, students know more than ever before what is happening in the greater world. Subsequently, they are pulled in many directions, both positive and negative. It is crucial for them to learn to think for themselves and make thoughtful decisions.

At the same time, some parents hover over their children, protect their every move, defend them when they are wrong, and try to catch them before every fall. This is a natural response that comes from love and the feeling of wanting the best for their children. It also comes from the recognition that through technology and the media, children are exposed to a rapidly changing world with many harsh realities. Yet, such parental actions may unintentionally inhibit children's development into responsive, responsible people. Children need the chance to develop autonomy and to make their own mistakes, experience the consequences of actions, take responsibility for their behavior, and recognize the effects of their actions on others.

In addition to overprotection, parental pressure to achieve may actually thwart the process of developing a sense of responsibility and independence. Madeleine Levine writes,

> [Children feel a] constant pressure to adopt a socially facile, highly competitive, performance-oriented, unblemished "self" that is promoted by omnipresent adults. This may encourage some children to perform at high levels, but more important, it also encourages dependency, depression, and a truncated sense of self in most children. . . .
>
> The reason that a well-developed sense of self is so critical is that in the desirable and inevitable absence of external support, a sense of self provides both a comfortable home base and an internal compass for navigating through life. (Levine, 2006, p. 65)

When teachers consider these influences on their students, they seek strategies to help them engage in meaningful ways to participate in the life of the classroom.

We believe that working together with parents as partners means listening to parent voices as well. Trust builds as parents and teachers get to know one another and share their goals for the students. Through building this trust, schools can work to treat all children fairly and ensure that consequences for behaviors are designed in the best interests of the students. Providing ongoing chances for students to take responsibility for their actions builds character and helps them develop a sense of belonging and responsiveness to others in the classroom.

LISTENING FOR STUDENTS' VOICES: HOW TO DO IT

Build Confidence to Participate

Teachers can use many strategies for building student participation in the classroom. Consider the following examples:

- Meera gave value to each voice in her classroom when she said to her students, "As your teacher I have a vested interest in hearing what each of you has to say."

- Ann used puppets to allow her second-grade students to try out different ways to express themselves.
- When Kendra (Grade 6) found her students were not used to expressing their ideas out loud in class discussions, she gave out sticky notes on which they could write their ideas. Then she read the ideas aloud. She did this until she created a trust level where they were comfortable sharing their opinions verbally without fear of being judged.

Similarly, in the first week of school, Kendra noticed that DeAngela (her only African American student) was extremely serious and withdrawn. Kendra described an incident in which DeAngela's status changed:

> I told my students, "If you've checked with three others before me, then you can come ask me. Then look to your classmates and ask so-and-so." Well, DeAngela was able to help on three different occasions. One thing DeAngela is really good at is following directions. So I suggested students check with DeAngela, and when I did she sat there for a minute; we had eye contact as if to say, "I know what you're doing." And she's sitting at a table with kids who have trouble understanding the directions. They're all going to her now, saying, "DeAngela, did you get the directions on that?" So, she had a really nice start of the year.

By noticing DeAngela's strength, Kendra was able to give her a new role that eventually shifted her status in the classroom. Her new status makes her a believable resource for other students.

For DeAngela and Arnoldo, speaking in class led to increasing levels of confidence and eventually to leadership. Arnoldo also shifted from shyness to confidence and later to leadership roles. With Arnoldo, Kendra said that she first found his "avenues of strength and then gave him chances for leadership." She noted, "He is feeling comfortable now, it's great; I think he's grown into himself."

In another example, Rafa, who was not one of Julia's best writers, was a bit of a joker. She had given the whole first-grade class an assignment to write an essay to enter into Macy's Earth Day Contest, and she encouraged all her students to be creative. Rafa wrote, "If my mom did not give me a bath every day, we could save water. If every time someone had a new baby, they planted a tree, there would be many forests." It was Rafa's unique first-grade voice that won the $5,000 scholarship from Macy's.

Having a voice in class is essential in a child's emerging sense of self and is an important element for creating identity safety for everyone in class. Teachers can encourage students to learn about and become aware of themselves and one another by giving them opportunities to express feelings and ideas and to take on leadership roles in their classrooms. These experiences can help prepare students to become leaders.

Evaluate Their Work Together

A common complaint from students about grading is expressed in the following manner: "Mrs. Washington gave me a bad grade," or "Mr. Smith should have given me an A." These comments reflect the belief that grades are given by teachers and received by students. This is the most common form of evaluation in schools. Important opportunities for teachers to learn about students' understanding and level of thinking can be lost through this top-down form of evaluation.

Not only is this information about students lost, but also this process fails to offer the students the chance to appreciate their understandings and recognize and correct their misunderstandings. If evaluation is done in a manner that permits students to review and improve their work, they will be more likely to retain the information and use it to connect it to new information. Some of the most important teaching and learning can occur during the process of teacher/student evaluation conferences.

Schools' usual focus on giving and getting grades is linked to an unspoken goal of identifying which students got things "right" instead of promoting high-level learning among all students. This has the effect of focusing on performance rather than on the process of learning. It encourages the belief that ability is a given rather than accomplished through effort.

One powerful way for teachers to listen to students and to support their efforts to learn is through the process of portfolio collections and evaluations. For example, when students systematically collect writing samples over the year and have opportunities to share their work and thinking with teachers, parents, and other students, their work and its quality becomes their own. They will be able to see progress and reflect on their efforts and growing knowledge. (See, for example, *Work Sampling System* by Meisels, Marsden, Jablon, Dorfman, & Dichtelmiller, 1998.)

Promote Student Creativity and Initiative

When teachers listen for students' voices, creativity and initiative can flourish. Natural curiosity and imagination are fostered when students are encouraged to draw on inner resources. Becki explained that when she was a principal, teachers worked together to help one student who was struggling:

> We analyzed Miguel's strengths and areas he needed to improve. It turned out he loved to write, and he loved computers. But he had been having a lot of trouble getting his work finished and getting along with his peers. I proceeded to get him a writing notebook. I told him that when he completed his work, he could write in that little booklet and then come to the office and use my computer to find pictures to go with his stories. Using my computer made him feel very important, and he was extremely careful to take good care of it. Within days that notebook was full of stories about animals together with pictures he found on the Internet and printed. His behavior improved, and so did his class work.

In Karen's fifth-grade class's photography project, students chose an area of interest, planned a complex project, and carried it out. She described how it strengthened academic skills, brought out their creativity, and helped them take responsibility for their learning:

> We had disposable cameras, and each table group got one. The students took turns taking it home to take five pictures of the most important things in their lives. Then we talked and did writing lessons around that. It was really cool. For one photo, Elena wrote an invitation to all of her previous teachers who were still at Hanover School, setting a date and time to meet in front of the school entry sign. She got all of us to line up, and she took a group picture of all the teachers she had had since kindergarten. And she thanked us for posing for the photo by giving us each a little red envelope with some chocolate money in it as a thank you from her on Chinese New Year. It's really nice that she is so thoughtful and she had planned it. Everyone was so touched and she orchestrated the whole thing.

Karen's particular strengths hinged around her ability to continually monitor students and nudge them to the next academic and behavioral levels. The Common Core State Standards delineate guidelines for students to increasingly develop their speaking abilities. She made sure to listen for students' voices and offer a range of speaking opportunities to encourage student confidence and leadership for students at all achievement and developmental levels.

CHALLENGES AND DILEMMAS

Teachers face several challenges when creating opportunities to listen to students as they participate in deciding how the classroom will operate, especially as the teachers make sure that every student has the chance to participate. The two challenges we will examine are

1. assigning classroom roles, and

2. listening for the voices of students who have difficulty self-regulating.

Assign Classroom Roles

One challenge with giving students more voice is how to assign classroom roles fairly. Ken talked about how he had his fourth-grade students help him identify the different classroom jobs that were needed. He described how he makes certain that each child takes a leadership role at some time during our learning. "I make certain that every child has a voice in the classroom." Students can help their teachers identify jobs that need to be done and a fair way to distribute the jobs.

Students served as line leaders, homework collectors, and greeters. Greeters were assigned to go up to any adult who entered the room and determine the purpose of that person's visit. While roles offer students a chance to shine and build autonomy, they can easily set up hierarchies in the classroom. Sometimes teachers inadvertently give more important roles to high-achieving students. Ken made sure that roles were flexible and all students got to experience some of the important classroom jobs.

Listen for the Voices of Students
Who Have Difficulty Self-Regulating

Some challenges arise for teachers when they want to promote the voices of students who have problems with impulse control, defiance, and working independently. These students not only continually disrupt classrooms but also undermine a teacher's efforts to give the entire class increasing levels of autonomy, because they abuse privileges and are continually pushing limits. Raymond, a third grader, had trouble starting his assignments and couldn't stay focused to complete his work. Janet, a second grader, could not stay in her seat and often abused the privilege of going to the restroom by staying out of class for long periods of time. Richard, a fifth grader, continually called out in class, challenging his teacher, even to the point of singing a little song: "I hate my teacher, I hate my teacher."

Their teachers grappled with the fact that they did not want to continually correct and criticize these students who actually needed a sense of autonomy and self-control as much as, or even more than, any other child in the class, because they were continually failing and having consequences for their behaviors that drummed in their lack of ability to manage themselves. The teachers worked with the school counselor to develop a positive behavior plan for each of these students. Each student's plan focused on monitoring behaviors and increasing levels of autonomy as successes were observed.

For Raymond, it involved shortening the assignments, giving him a choice of how many math problems he would complete, and increasing the number as he was becoming successful. For Janet, it was allowing her to take two-minute relaxation breaks in the library, which was next to her classroom. She could take the breaks as frequently as she needed them. At first her teacher observed that she seemed to be bouncing into her seat and then running to take another break. However, over time, she was limited to three breaks a day to relax and eventually was allowed only one. After a period of months, she took her breaks in the classroom though she rarely needed them.

Richard's teacher began working with the school counselor to find ways to manage his anger. For him, the key was building a relationship with and developing trust in his teacher. She worked to find ways to give him positive leadership roles in the classroom and to begin to alter his sense of himself as a bully. Meanwhile, the counselor invited him to help her lead the social skills groups for the first graders. In each case, the teachers developed explicit systems for monitoring and worked to avoid continually correcting the students.

Sometimes, when a student has totally lost control, the first step is transitioning an unacceptable behavior into an acceptable one. One principal found herself crawling on the rug with a first grader, Ramon, whose medication had worn off, causing him to run wild in the library. She convinced Ramon to come to the computer lab, where he shifted his energy to work on a reading program and sat mesmerized for over an hour. There, she was able to talk with him calmly so he could reflect on his behavior and articulate what was expected.

In his book, *Lost at School* (2008), Ross Greene provides a new framework for helping the most challenging students by teaching them "lagging skills." Greene says rather than looking at these students as unmotivated, manipulative, and always wanting their own way—or simply as mentally ill—teachers need to recognize that these students actually want to be successful and would do well if they could. Greene proposes identifying the specific skills that are lagging. Some examples of lagging skills will be very familiar to teachers: managing the transition from one activity to another, maintaining focus, expressing needs, appreciating how behavior is affecting others, empathizing with another's point of view, entering groups and connecting with people.

Greene says that once the lagging skill is identified, the next step is to have the student help define the problem. Then the teacher empathizes with the student and extends an invitation to collaboratively find solutions to the problem. The student has a stake in the solution, because the student helped formulate the plan.

Even the most challenged students benefit from practicing autonomy, learning social skills, and actively participating in finding solutions to the difficulties they are facing. This collaborative approach is a key to supporting a pathway back to success in school. A teacher in an identity safe classroom recognizes that this is not a simple process or a quick road to improvement but is rather one of many misses and multiple tries over time to make desired changes.

PUTTING LISTENING FOR STUDENTS' VOICES INTO PRACTICE

1. Reflect on your personal experience with speaking in a group, both when you were a student and in the present.
   - Do you feel free to speak up in groups?

   - What allows you to feel safe to speak up in one place but not another?

2. Consider your students who come from backgrounds different from yours.
   - How might their experience be like yours, and how might it be different?

   - Are any of your student's voices silenced, perhaps not by you, but by past experiences of being marginalized?

3. Observe the speaking patterns in your classroom.
   - Make a simple tally of who is speaking in the group. Mark the initials of each child who speaks. We suggest you do this more than one time.

(Continued)

(Continued)

- Analyze your data by asking yourself the following questions:
  - How many students in the class spoke out loud in the discussion?

  - Who spoke more than once?

  - Who did not speak at all?

  - What were the social identities of those who spoke and those who did not?

  - How can you extend opportunities to ensure everyone gets a chance to speak?

  - What kinds of encouragement can you give right in the moment as students speak?

Teaching for Understanding

4

WHY TEACHING FOR UNDERSTANDING?

Take a minute to watch a television program in a language you do not understand. How did it feel? Did you feel lost or disconnected? Did you have a sense of disorientation that sent you on a goose chase to grasp for meaning? Instead of making meaning of what is going on, did you feel frustrated, as if you were spinning in circles?

Becki discovered that even missing a key word can lead to the same feeling:

> As a fluent Spanish speaker, I observed a hands-on science lesson in a Spanish immersion classroom. However, there was one word that I did not understand, and I could not make sense of what was going on. The word was *paper clip*. That was a word I learned in Nicaragua, where, as in many other Spanish-speaking countries, they just borrowed the English word *clip*. In other Spanish-speaking countries, the word is *sujetapapeles*. What struck me was how lost I became without that singular key word, even though I understood all the other words and even though there were paper clips all around, as the children were using them to measure. When they told me the meaning of the word, suddenly it all made sense to me, I *understood*.

Understanding is the core of engagement. The words *teaching* and *learning* are used together for just that reason. You may be teaching, but are they learning? Understanding is the bridge between teaching and learning.

Teaching for understanding is a way of teaching that emphasizes meaning-making. Viewed as the bridge between teaching and learning, it can be accomplished through a range of strategies that include the simplest way of explaining an idea in your own words, to testing a theory or discovering one through a hand-on science experiment, to applying a math concept in a whole new context. Good teaching culminates with the important strategy "checking for understanding." Without true understanding of what it means to find a ratio, or a main idea in a text, or the meaning of the word *ecology*, learning remains at the most superficial level, that of accumulating facts. Applying new knowledge, synthesizing that knowledge with other knowledge, analyzing the information, and evaluating the ideas in relation to other information is beyond the reach of students who can merely spout the answers but cannot explain the ideas in their own words.

This difference between teaching facts and teaching for understanding is exacerbated in the current educational climate, which emphasizes test scores as the main purpose of teaching (Darling-Hammond, 2010). Teachers find that they do not have the time to teach a concept deeply before they must move on in order to squeeze all standards in before the month of standardized testing rolls around. This has the most detrimental effect on schools with many low-achieving students, who may not have the resources of tutors, mentors, or parent support to learn what they did not learn in class. When teachers rush to jam in all the standards, many of the concepts, particularly in math, are not sufficiently understood before new concepts are introduced. Math consists of a series of concepts built one upon the other. Students' mathematical proficiency will decrease as they move through the grades if they have not learned the prior concepts.

However, some of the greatest damage is for students who are unable to pass algebra, the gateway to higher level math and ultimately college readiness, because they lack proficiency in basic math skills. The gateway to higher learning shuts down for many students from urban settings who must repeat remedial courses numerous times when they get to college (Boaler & Staples, 2008). Ultimately many of these students give up on higher education because their math scores are so low. Similarly, in the area of literacy, students who do not understand how to write independently are not able to write a well-structured analytic research paper, the foundation of college studies. Teaching for understanding is crucial in closing the gaps in opportunity and achievement.

The Common Core State Standards aim to help students achieve high levels of performance with relevant and rigorous curricula linked to real-world situations, which prepare students for success in college and a future career. These new standards are designed to foster critical thinking. Students are given greater exposure to informational texts in elementary school and explicitly learn and practice expository writing skills. Curricula designed to meet these standards will shift the focus to teaching for understanding. The learning strategies we describe below will help teachers incorporate the Common Core.

TEACHING FOR UNDERSTANDING: HOW TO DO IT

Prepare Students for New Activities

The first step in promoting student understanding is to tell students what is happening and why. This approach includes sharing daily schedules, preparing them in advance for a change of activities, and orienting them to an upcoming lesson. All students benefit from having schedules posted, changes explained, and help in understanding and anticipating the activities of the day. This is particularly important for students who lack executive functioning skills, including those with ADHD, autism, and other learning disabilities.

As a young teacher, Dorothy had a struggle each day in getting her class of four- and five-year-olds to leave the play yard to return to class. The transition from happy outdoor times always ended with sad children leaving the play yard. One day she learned that giving her students a 5-minute warning and reminding them of the snack waiting for them in the classroom changed everything. Students knew what was coming and could take their one last swing, throw the ball, or climb to the top of the structure.

Though this is now a commonly practiced strategy to get students to comply with teachers' wishes, it is more than that. Telling students what is going to happen gives them a sense of agency and belonging. Students who know what is happening are students who are thinking about themselves as active participants in the classroom community.

Importantly, this same strategy applies to academic lessons and activities. Teachers can talk with students about the purpose of studying an upcoming unit in social studies. For example, they can have the students work cooperatively on writing a newspaper that covers the events described in the social studies unit. This project engages the students in the activity as they build on what they know from their own experiences and helps them think about what they might learn. This discussion can include a time for teachers to invite students into thinking about the questions and ideas they may encounter and to consider how these relate to their own lives. And teachers can informally assess what students already know and what their level of interest in the topic is, so teachers can provide meaningful support to enhance learning.

Though these orientation conversations take some time, the gain in student interest in and identification with the activity will lead to more engaged learners. Nothing can deflate engagement more than asking students to read the next chapter and answer each question "just because it is next."

Make Instructions Clear

One of the first aspects of making instruction accessible to each student is clearly explaining instructional objectives. Many schools now have the teaching standards posted and instructional objectives delineated. Identity safe teachers take the extra time to not only explicitly state goals for learning in terms that students understand, but also explain the relevance of the learning to the students' lives. Students are more likely to engage with content when they understand the purpose of the activity, why it is important to learn, and what they will be able to do by the end of the lesson.

Another path to student understanding and engagement is to ensure that all students understand the directions (Costa, 2008). Ann had so many English learners in her second grade that she worried that children would be unsure what to do or were afraid to ask and would be stymied in completing class work. Ann presented instructions in several modalities:

> I consistently try to make instructions clear by giving them orally, modeling them, writing them on the board in a color-coded way, and finally checking for understanding. I usually model partner activities with our invisible student, George (named after my favorite uncle). George is always the person who helps demonstrate what to do or not do, and George always gets a chuckle. The students love to play along and will often tell me what George is doing, saying, or thinking! In this way, humor is added and everyone becomes my partner.

In addition Ann checked for understanding by asking students to restate the instructions for the others. Students were also taught to consult one another before asking the teacher. "I always ask if anyone has questions and often offer a 'clinic' on the carpet for those who want more clarification."

Monitor Students and Teach Them to Reflect on Their Learning

Monitoring refers to teaching students how to self-assess and involves teachers continually checking on and providing specific feedback to students. According to Marzano (1998), clear and constructive feedback to students about their progress in meeting instructional goals is one of the most effective and powerful tools in instruction.

Karen had several simple techniques to monitor her students' progress and offer feedback. She asked them to write main ideas on sticky notes as they read. When she circulated, she could easily assess if they understood the reading. She asked for a quick thumbs up if they understood, thumbs down if they did not, and a wavy hand if they were not sure. Karen also showed them how to monitor their own progress, seek help, find the definitions for vocabulary words, and reflect on experiences.

Ken commented that providing immediate, specific feedback during instruction was the most effective way to correct errors and affirm that students grasped the content. When Becki was a principal, she bought an individual white board for each student. The students used the white boards to do simple activities during instruction, and this allowed the teachers to quickly scan the white boards and affirm that students understood a particular concept. One new teacher became enamored with using the white boards. When Becki observed him, she saw students calling out to him "Mr. Marquez, Mr. Marquez, look at my work." While the students were excited and motivated, it made the classroom chaotic, because they were all calling out. Later, he came up with a more effective system. He taught the students to raise their white boards silently, and he gave a thumbs up when their answer was correct. If more work was needed, he made his fingers into a *T* for "try it one more time."

Provide Equal Opportunity to Access Learning

To create an identity safe classroom, teachers have the added challenge of providing differentiated instruction while keeping in mind the goal of promoting equal status among students. While most classrooms have a wide range of learners at different levels, the incremental view of intelligence suggests that whether students are labeled highly gifted or learning disabled, their potentials are not predetermined. Differentiation strategies will be covered in the "Challenging Curriculum" chapter in Part V.

Introduction and Closure of Lessons

Julia, a new fourth-grade teacher, was searching for a way to help her students retain new information. She told her mentor that often she covered certain material many times, but the students just could not seem to remember it. Her mentor suggested a way to use the processes of introducing and closing each lesson as a way to help students incorporate new information and ideas. Her mentor explained that the purpose of introducing each lesson is to link the students' prior knowledge to the lesson. Brain researchers have found that if new knowledge is hooked onto previous knowledge, it is more likely that the new knowledge will be remembered (Sousa, 2006). The process of bringing closure to the end of a lesson is more than the teacher recapping the lesson. Closure includes involving all children in summarizing the entire lesson for themselves to incorporate the new ideas into their own thinking.

CHALLENGES AND DILEMMAS

We have selected one significant challenge all teachers face in teaching for understanding. It is the challenge of ensuring that each of the students has really understood the information, concepts, and objectives of a lesson.

How Do You Know if the Students Understand?

During whole-class teaching, students can appear to be sitting quietly and listening, but how do teachers know if the students really comprehend the concept? So often, rote instruction allows students to find the answer in the book without really getting what the teacher is teaching. When students are spoon-fed instruction, they often want to jump over meaning to get to the "right" answer.

There is a series of questions teachers can ask themselves when considering whether students understand. What makes this content relevant to the student? Does the student have the prior knowledge to understand how this new concept fits into a body of knowledge? Are there cultural differences that might contribute to the student's understanding? Is the English comprehensible? Does the student know why this information is even being taught?

PUTTING TEACHING FOR UNDERSTANDING INTO PRACTICE

1. Consider your personal experience.
   - What engaged you as a learner?

   - What did your teachers do or not do to challenge your mind, encourage your thinking, and bring out your ideas?

   - Did you feel a sense of connection as a student, or did you feel marginalized?

2. Observe a student who has a different cultural background from yours.
   - Consider the way he or she engages with the learning. Be sure not to stereotype the child or generalize his experiences to others with similar backgrounds.

   - Ask yourself the following questions:
     ○ How do I feel when I am teaching this child?

     ○ What strengths does he or she bring from her home life?

(Continued)

(Continued)

○ Do any of her learning behaviors make me uncomfort-able? For example, do I feel she is too loud or too quiet?

○ What assumptions am I making about the reasons for her behavior? For example, do I think she is seeking attention or purposely disrupting?

○ What external factors might be influencing her behavior?

○ Are there any alternative explanations that I have not con-sidered?

○ How can I respond differently?

○ Am I making similar assumptions about other students' behaviors?

Focus on Cooperation

5

WHY FOCUS ON COOPERATION?

As John Dewey demonstrated in his lab school at the University of Chicago (1896–1903), classrooms can be places where individual students develop their full capacities through the "active participation in the education of one by the others" (Mayhew & Edwards, 1936). In his view, the role that students play in the development of one another is the foundation for ensuring the social good, through the social relationships experienced in school as community.

It is important to create cooperative communities in schools to support the development of individual students' capacities and fully meet their developmental needs. When students cooperate, their learning is increased, and they develop a positive attachment to school. Identity safe classrooms promote a feeling in which all are working together for positive goals, and there are no winners and losers. Instead, each student's success is the success of the whole.

The capacity to work together has been a hallmark of humanity and the basis for building a civil society. In the earliest human groups, survival was dependent on every member cooperating. The history of human achievements is the result of people continually building on the work of those who came before them. Now, more than ever in history, the future of our planet is contingent on peoples of many backgrounds and nations collaborating.

To help students learn how to work cooperatively, teachers can plan activities that require students to listen to others, provide help in accomplishing agreed-upon goals, and show concern for others' ideas and feelings. This is a developmental process. Students will make mistakes while they are learning it, just as students who are learning to read make mistakes. When students engage in cooperative activities, teachers can help

41

them evaluate whether they were empathetic to other students, listened well and included others' ideas, and balanced the need to dominate or control the situation with true engagement. These skills need to be taught, developed, and regularly practiced.

Many schools use character education programs to help students learn to work cooperatively. One school held an assembly and put up posters to promote respect, cooperation, and trust. The teachers opted for this simple method over a more comprehensive character education curriculum, because they feared they would not have time to implement it *and* to cover the basics required to raise test scores. Yet, the students at that school persisted in calling each other terrible names and even called a parent "fat" when she came to campus. Clearly, from the students' perspective, these values were not part of the fabric of their school, even though these values may have been posted and promoted at school assemblies. Cooperation and other ethical behaviors are not learned through exhortation but have to be taught, modeled, and practiced.

Teachers who structure lessons based on student cooperation cultivate empathy and a kind of shared leadership that allows students to develop their strengths, appreciate what each group member has to offer, and work together for a goal. Some students complain that when teachers assign a group project, a few of the students do all the work. In other cases, teachers are discouraged about the tendency for some students to take over while others kick back, so they abandon these kinds of group activities. However, a way to ensure that students participate fairly and gain from the experience is to teach collaborative skills in advance. By carefully crafting learning opportunities that are not based on high-stakes outcomes and competition, lessons can be designed to focus on both the process of working together and the final product. Students will become successful if the collaborative activities are structured in such a way that the success of the activity is contingent on student cooperation. Students living in a cooperative, helpful class are more likely to feel identity safe as they develop a sense of belonging and contribute to their class community.

FOCUS ON COOPERATION: HOW TO DO IT

Work With a Partner

Providing opportunities for students to work in partnerships on meaningful tasks is an important way to teach them to cooperate while promoting their intellectual development. Meera did not leave student interactions to chance. In facilitating cooperative group work for her fifth-grade class, Meera carefully observed the student learning process as well as the products of the learning. For example, she observed Moiz and Jaime as they worked as partners. She had previously noted the tendency for Moiz to dominate his peers and knew that this quality would not serve him in his life. She also noticed that Jaime tended to allow others to push him around. On this occasion, she challenged Moiz when he was not giving his partner, Jaime, enough of a chance to do his own thinking. After speaking privately to each boy, Meera observed Jaime work up his courage to boldly tell Moiz, "Please give me a chance to try."

Meera commented that Carlota, the new student from Peru, worked well with her partner to negotiate a fair way of taking turns. She specifically praised Carlotta to be sure that Carlotta would know that this skill was valued. Meera provided many varied opportunities for group work, including partner reading, a group project to write a colonial newspaper, science experiments, and math games. Each time, she circulated around the class watching the dynamics of the different partnerships. In a whole-class debrief, she asked students to reflect on their work together, saying, "How were you working together with your partner?" She considered this reflective practice extremely important for group work in order to ensure that no one child dominated or did all or most of the work while others did nothing.

The students in Karen's fifth-grade class had similar issues in learning to work together successfully. When Tina and Armando worked together, Karen stayed close to them. Tina had been identified as a gifted student; however, her rapid-fire responses, when contrasted with Armando's timid ones, were potentially problematic. For Armando, Tina's behavior obviously inhibited his confidence. This dynamic tended to make Tina appear obnoxious and overbearing. Karen wanted Armando to try harder, and she wanted Tina to learn patience. She placed them together only after she taught the whole class about the steps involved in working successfully with partners. She did this by having the whole class discuss the qualities they wanted in a class partner. They role-played, and then they tried partner work a few times. Because of this preparation, when Tina and Armando worked together, Armando was able to tell Tina how he felt, and Karen was able to mediate, when needed.

Young students can learn to work cooperatively, too. Becki had her first-grade students help edit each other's writing. She did this with the whole group by teaching them three steps. First, she asked a student to read his writing to the whole class. Then the class would discuss three things about the writing: one thing they liked, one question, and one suggestion to improve the writing. They role-played this process with the whole group to teach them the steps. Then, she taught them to think about how they worked together.

Rather than using generic terms like *easy* or *hard* or *good* or *bad*, the class brainstormed descriptive words that would help with this reflection process. Becki also taught them to look for parts of the writing, using examples from previous lessons she had taught, like descriptive words or main idea. Only after many whole-group sessions did the students begin their partner work. Becki was so pleased when one of her students, Luis, told his partner, "What I liked about your story was that it had a beginning, middle, and end."

In each of these examples, the teachers explicitly taught the students how to work with a partner. The whole class discussed the qualities they wanted in a class partner. They role-played, and then they tried it a few times. Whenever they worked with partners, the teacher debriefed the students after the activity to discover how well they had worked together. When students reflected on how they worked together, they were able to improve their cooperative skills.

Similarly, when working in larger groups, teachers can lay out the steps for the process. The students can identify all aspects of working together on a group effort. Some of the most exciting learning opportunities are whole-class efforts where groups research different topics that, when combined like pieces of a puzzle, fit together into a unified whole. For example, students can create a class book on the rain forest to which every student contributes, design a gold rush simulation, or invent math games or puzzles for other groups. These types of activities motivate, apply new learning, and allow students to enjoy the fruit of cooperation. Taught in the context of empathy and positive communication, students can learn to appreciate what each child has to contribute.

When some fourth graders made a video about why school was important and how dropping out of school can lead to negative results, each team worked on different parts of the video. Each section required creativity (creative problem solving and perspective taking), writing a storyboard (sequencing skills), script writing (expository writing), acting (oral communication), and finding a way for each student to participate (cooperating).

Kurt was a student in that fourth-grade class who often did not focus, never completed any work, and could not get along in groups. Yet he became the leader of the rap about staying in school. He did the vocal rhythm with popping sounds for the finale of the video. For Kurt, this was the first time he felt good about a positive contribution to the group, and it was also the first time for the others to appreciate his talents. His schoolwork started improving little by little after that first hint of success. These types of experiences can lead students to a more engaged and successful year in school.

Class Teamwork

As described earlier, it is usually most beneficial to begin teaching cooperation in partnerships, even in dyads, before engaging larger groups of students in working together. This will help students focus their efforts and encourage them to really engage in the task. (Their partners are not likely to let them off easily.) After some success with partnerships, working as a team in class can have some especially effective social benefits as teachers monitor and model showing concern, listening carefully, and helpfulness.

One way to begin is to help students focus on concepts involved in working together toward a shared goal. Meera used her circle time to prepare students for their upcoming work together. She asked each of the students to define the words *cooperation* and *teamwork*, giving examples from their personal experience. They discussed the contrast between cooperation and competition, and the ways competition can increase the chances for students to feel excluded.

Ann described how she teaches cooperation in her second-grade class:

> We teach cooperation explicitly, how to agree, how to share materials, and how to support each other. After the activity, we reflect on what worked and didn't work in their groups. These conversations give them ownership for their success. Working with others is a skill we learn about all year.

And for fun and a sense of team identity, Ann helped her students build a class team, renaming Room Fourteen to Room Fourteam.

Focus on Social Understanding

Every cooperative learning lesson can include both a social *and* an academic goal (Child Development Project, 1996, 1997). Social goals are chosen by the teacher or suggested by the students, based on a skill that students need to develop. The social goal is focused on a specific area of growth like sharing materials, listening to one another, or ensuring each team member has a chance to participate equally. Both the social goal and the academic goal are presented at the beginning of the lesson. After the lesson, students respond to reflection questions. First, students have a closure question that asks them to reflect on everything learned in the lesson. This helps students retain the learning of the entire lesson.

The second question is related to the social goal. If the social goal was to work together, a simple question like, "How did your group work together?" will suffice. Or, the question can target a particular aspect of the way they worked together. "Did each student in your group participate fully?" Or, "Did your team work together without bickering or conflict?" Norms are set to ensure students reflect on their own behavior rather than blame or personally attack other members of the group. Identity safe teachers validate self-perceptive comments.

When a student identifies a weakness the class needs to work on, the teacher acknowledges the value of recognizing where they need to improve. If a student comments on how the group or class improved, the teacher celebrates the growth. Based on how the students feel the class did in meeting a social goal, they can either continue to improve on that goal or identify a new one for a future lesson. Students can become quite facile with self-reflection using this process over the course of a year. This tool is also useful for beginning teachers working on classroom management. A teacher can give clear expectations for behavior, and the students can continually hone their skills. This simple process takes no more than five minutes out of the lesson but has great promise for creating well-managed classrooms and a true sense of identity safety among the students (Child Development Project, 1996, 1997).

Encourage Spontaneous Helping and Caring

In identity safe classrooms, teachers use cooperative activities and other collaborative instructional formats for differentiating their instruction to meet the needs of different learners. This chapter, "Focus on Cooperation," is placed in the Child-Centered Teaching section to signal that teaching students to cooperate has important intellectual *and* social goals for student development. One of the most important social outcomes of focusing on cooperation in the classroom is helping students develop abilities in spontaneous helping, showing concern for one another, and careful listening to learn from one another.

Working toward these goals for cooperation is not only a nice way to improve the tone in the classroom but is also an essential step in the process of helping all students gain a sense of identity safety in the classroom. Through our research with the Stanford Integrated Schools Project (SISP), we learned that the ability to work cooperatively is linked to every aspect of student identity safety, including an authentic sense of belonging (from learning how to connect with others), autonomy (as students help one another, they become more independent), and commitment to and engagement in learning.

One example may help to demonstrate this. When Dorothy, a teacher educator, visited a low-income, urban school, she was struck with the top-down control that teachers had over the students. For example, as a small group of sixth graders left the gym for their classroom, boys on one side, girls on the other side, one student dropped her notebook. The contents of the notebook spread over the hallway. The student and her classmates looked stricken. No one stooped to pick things up. Instead, all of them looked at the teacher to see what was going to happen. The teacher nodded permission and a couple of girls rushed to help the girl who was still upset.

This quick incident tells us a lot about the teacher–student relationships in this school. The policies and practices of this school are based on the assumption that students cannot be trusted to think for themselves and to act in a responsive manner to their classmates. Yet, as soon as the students leave the school, they are on their own in a complex, dynamic city where few people are looking out for them. Students living in these harsh environments may need, more than anything, support to recognize what is going on, to learn how to act to be safe, and to take care of their families and friends.

CHALLENGES AND DILEMMAS

Getting started is the biggest challenge for using strategies to promote cooperation among students.

Getting Started: Knowing How

Though aspects of cooperative learning have become common practice in some classrooms, we hope this chapter will help teachers consider the wide possibilities for deepening understanding, both social and intellectual, that students can gain from meaningful cooperative learning engagements. Few teachers have been taught how to include practices that promote cooperation among students. And many relegate cooperation to "cooperative-learning" lessons, which may or may not be connected to other experiences and issues in the classroom. These decontextualized cooperative-learning lessons are not likely to influence future student behavior unless teachers help students make the connection from the lesson to other situations in the classroom. Some teachers, given the press of time, believe that taking time for students to learn how to work together and to help one another is not worth it.

But, we see that cooperation among students is central to the process of really creating an identity safe classroom. Like learning math concepts, learning to cooperate takes guidance and practice. Mistakes will be made, but they, too, can contribute to student learning.

Dorothy worked with a teacher in a low-income, urban school where the level of discipline and learning were both low. The teacher's approach was strict, top-down discipline for his third-grade class. More time was spent on correcting students than in engaging them in learning. When Dorothy suggested the teacher let the students help one another in reading a text and discussing its meaning, the teacher replied, "They don't know how to work together."

This response suggests the teacher may not recognize that it is part of his role to foster attitudes of cooperation and teach the skills that go with it. With his guidance, students can gain skills in cooperating. Although cooperation is part of many cultures, and many students are used to cooperating in their families, if students have not been taught how to do it at school and have seen classroom life only as an experience of competition for grades and status, they may need explicit teaching. The focus on helping students to learn in a cooperative environment accomplishes many things. It supports student learning by giving them the chance to help one another. It can create a real sense of belonging, as students learn they can help someone else. And, finally, it underlines that learning is a process that involves many efforts, ideas, and perspectives.

To start, it helps to not think of cooperation as an add-on and to try to weave a sense of cooperation and helping into everyday life. By beginning simply, both students and teacher will build skills. Even practicing spelling lists can be done in partnerships. Levels of cooperation will gradually increase when it is practiced regularly and supported by the teacher. Try to use learning activities that are improved by students working together on them. Increasing cooperation will increase learning levels and make the classroom a more intellectually dynamic, pleasurable, and welcoming place for everyone.

**PUTTING FOCUS ON
COOPERATION INTO PRACTICE**

1. Begin with your own experiences.
   - How do feel about cooperating and collaborating?

   - Are cooperative activities familiar to you from your family or from your school experience?

   - What are the most effective cooperation strategies you have already incorporated into your classroom?

2. Thinking of each of your students, consider cooperative activities from the diverse perspectives they may have.
   - What might influence their interest in and skills with cooperative learning?

   - Have they done this before?

(Continued)

(Continued)

- Do they feel a sense of belonging enough to trust others in a group project?

- Is this something their families may value, or not? Do families expect boys and girls to have the same roles as leaders?

- How do you respond to differences in expectations between school and families?

3. How do you make time for cooperative activities?

- What other barriers do you find to helping your students learn to cooperate?

- How do you overcome them?

Classroom Autonomy

6

WHY PROMOTE CLASSROOM AUTONOMY?

The sense of being able to manage ourselves and our lives and the capacity to influence the world around us is a basic human need (Deci & Flaste, 1996).

Becki described how important autonomy was to her as a child:

> When I think about my own childhood, I remember most vividly when I could do something "all by myself." I remember the first book that I could read all by myself, *The Cat in the Hat Comes Back.* I even remember where I was sitting when I read the book. I also remember when I rode a bike for the first time. It was a big ugly rusty brown boy's bike and I kept falling over. And then all of a sudden, I was riding, wobbling just a bit, but I managed to cross the patio in front of our house and come to a stop without falling.
>
> I love to ask students to remember learning to do something that at first seemed impossible and really hard, and then after trying over and over, they could finally do it. Many also describe learning to ride a bike, others have described learning to speak English, mastering a video game, and solving a hard math problem. Every child can identify with the challenge of effort and the joy of mastery.

Developing autonomy means allowing children not only to function independently but also to bring into play all aspects of themselves—both what they have in common with other children and what is unique to each of them. Teachers in the IDS study group (author Becki Cohn-Vargas's identity safety study group) wanted to encourage students to feel comfortable bringing their whole selves into interactions with adults and peers. When they talked about the meaning of autonomy, they agreed that even in an autonomous classroom, students do not have complete freedom to do anything they want, because students need structure and limits (Deci & Flaste, 1996). Rather, autonomy refers to students making choices and taking increasing responsibility over their lives (Sylwester, 2007). They work *with* the teacher to set classroom rules and norms, to plan activities, and to reflect on their progress.

In a classroom that promotes autonomy, students learn to manage their own feelings, problems, and behavior in general. Ultimately, when the teacher promotes autonomy, he shows that he trusts the students, so they can respond by rising to those expectations. One can say that trust between the teacher and students is the foundation of a truly autonomous classroom.

Another aspect of autonomy is self-regulation. The capacity to monitor their behavior gradually evolves for most students as they develop, but for some, impulse control does not emerge easily. Pierre, a child who lacked impulse control, might haul off and slug another child because, as he put it, "That kid looked at me funny." Students like Pierre have to be taught explicitly how to regulate their behavior along with strategies for pausing and choosing an appropriate and effective response. Helping each child learn to control his own responses is also a part of an identity safe autonomous classroom (Barkley, 2005).

With increased autonomy, children can come to develop a sense of self-efficacy, a sense of being capable. Self-efficacy means that they have ownership of their choices and can positively impact outcomes in their environment. Along with a sense of self-efficacy, children develop a sense of agency, the capacity to act in an appropriate and effective way. This sense of agency leads to a feeling that "I can make something happen." Children who do not have a sense of agency feel like "things happen to them," and these children are much more likely than others to be negatively influenced and manipulated (Levine, 2006). Children also need to sort through the multitude of opportunities they have as well as learn about boundaries and the many things that they cannot control. They need to begin to understand where their actions fit amid the confluence of swirling opportunities, limitations, and illusions of both power and powerlessness.

In their book, *Raising Self-Reliant Kids in a Self-Indulgent World*, H. Stephen Glenn and Jane Nelsen (1989) discussed the effects of feeling powerless and a lack of autonomy, saying,

> One characteristic of people who tend to get into trouble is their perception that they have little or no power to affect what happens

to them. They put their faith in fate or luck and are frequently impotent in the face of choices. . . . Such people take one of three paths through life: (1) they continually feel depressed at their failure in finding success and happiness outside themselves, (2) they run on a treadmill while harboring the hope that someday they will find fulfillment out there, or (3) they live a life of rebellion, seeking a false sense of power. (p. 119)

In contrast, according to the authors, the behavior of people with a strong sense of self-efficacy is a result of their internal decisions to take appropriate action.

Having a sense of autonomy in the classroom fosters intrinsic motivation in students. Becki reports,

I learned many things about intrinsic motivation from my own children. My daughter thrived on assignments and projects that allowed her to choose and enhance her creative energy, whether it was making a recipe for friendship or simply writing her own word problems. It launched her creativity and to this day, she is finding her own ingenious solutions to problems. My son, who struggled with writing, overcame his initial blocks when he was able to write his own poetry in fourth grade and later he became a prolific writer when he was encouraged to choose his topics. He even wrote his own sequel to *Macbeth* that I proudly had bound in leather.

Deci and Ryan (1985) found that students in classrooms that supported autonomy had higher self-esteem, were more creative, and had more intrinsic motivation than those in classrooms where teachers were more directive and controlling. Children who experience increasing levels of autonomy develop a sense of agency, self-efficacy, and intrinsic motivation. They feel that their actions matter and that they can choose effective ways to behave and interact in the world.

CLASSROOM AUTONOMY: HOW TO DO IT

Offer Choices

In our SISP study, the teachers whose classrooms scored higher on the identity safety scale tended to give their students more choices than the other teachers. Choice can be as simple as having specific options for how to complete an activity, while in other cases, the choices are more open-ended. Students may choose the topic to study, such as selecting an event during the Civil War to write a report about or choosing to use a particular genre of writing, such as a poem or essay. In other cases, the choice may be in the format: When studying the rain forest, students may choose to write a story, make a multimedia presentation, create a work of art, or design an interactive web page. Autonomy is even promoted with small decisions: Teachers might ask, "Shall we do this now or later?" or "Which book do you want me to read aloud?" When meaningful choices are offered, students feel included and are invited to express their opinions and preferences. For classwide decisions, students can work together to decide whether to vote or come to consensus. They will need the chance to discuss a fair way to decide which approach to take. Offering choice has many positive benefits. Students learn how to make decisions and wise choices. They also feel more engaged in the activities and feel ownership of the outcomes. Research has demonstrated that opportunities for choice foster and enhance intrinsic motivation (Deci & Flaste, 1996).

Sometimes students enter a classroom without much experience with being given choices. They may be used to others doing the thinking and decision making for them. They may have an attitude of "Just tell me what to do." They may have never been given the chance to form their own opinions or think for themselves. In an identity safe classroom, the teacher teaches the skill of choosing incrementally. She may discuss the concept of good judgment or how an opinion is formulated. She recognizes that some of her students may be accustomed to being controlled, and she made need to be patient and understanding with a student who always says "I don't know" in response to a choice question. She may begin by offering a choice between two simple things: "Do you want to use the red or the blue paper?" Gradually the teacher can offer increasingly complex choices. In time, students will take pride in their role in making choices and in shaping the life of the classroom.

Build Self-Awareness and Self-Monitoring

Building the metacognitive skills of self-awareness and self-monitoring calls for students to have opportunities to reflect on their thinking and consider their goals for learning and their lives. Students need instruction in self-monitoring both during and at the end of an experience. Meera shared her method for building self-awareness in relation to the learning goals of her students:

> In the beginning of the year, I have students set goals for themselves. We revisit these goals and check them to make sure we are on track. This helps students be a part of their learning process.

In planning units, I also use the KWL chart [highlighting what they K—Know, W—Want to know, and L—Learned] to see what students know and what they want to learn. . . . Then the kids can say, "Oh, this is an area I need to work on."

Teachers use many ways to teach metacognitive skills for planning and self-monitoring. Planning charts on the walls can be used to outline student ideas for how to complete class projects. Science journals can be used to allow students to write what they hope to get out of an experiment and then document their findings. Individuals, partners, groups, or the whole class can create action plans in various ways. When a teacher is explicit about what students are to do, it helps them monitor their behavior and manage their time. For example, Karen asked her fifth-grade students to stop what they were doing, and then she told them to mentally plan what they wanted to accomplish in the next 20 minutes of their writing time. The students stopped for several minutes to think about how they were working toward completing their assignment. Karen explained that initially she teaches the steps for self-monitoring. Over the course of the year, she reminds students to self-monitor. As they become more competent, she reduces the number of reminders.

Foster Students' Responsibility for Their Behavior

Student self-management is another important component of autonomy. Karen told the IDS study group that one year her fifth-grade class needed explicit instructions. At the beginning of the school year, she even had to tell them exactly where they needed to turn their heads to face someone who was speaking. Over the year, she gradually weaned them from these cues, but she was overt as she did it, highlighting the behavior after they had demonstrated it without her cues.

Ken described how teachers need to help students learn to make their own decisions and take responsibility for their actions:

Autonomy begins with a teacher/facilitator who sets high expectations for student behaviors and follows up on those expectations. Students need to develop autonomy in and out of the classroom. They must be given the opportunity to make decisions. They need to learn from and live with the decisions they make.

Teachers find ways to foster classroom autonomy by helping students learn to take responsibility for their actions. This must be done differently depending on the age of the students. Though Ann had different goals for her second graders than Karen and Meera had for their fifth graders, each provided a level of support, so students could gradually increase responsibility for their behavior. When some students needed more support than others, these teachers found ways to provide it either privately or in front of the class in ways that did not single out any student.

For example, fourth grader Bobby was getting into frequent fights. He was remorseful each time; yet, in the moment, he would forget. The principal asked him to identify something that he could do to avoid getting into fights. He came up with the idea of doing volunteer work in a classroom for special needs students. So, he helped feed a severely disabled student. The special education teacher discovered Bobby had a gift of communicating with a boy who did not speak and rarely responded to anyone. This was a mutually beneficial relationship that astonished all the adults who knew Bobby and served to change his view of himself.

Foster Students' Responsibility for Their Learning

Karen viewed the process of her fifth-grade students' learning to think for themselves as cumulative. She applauded when one of her students learned how to "stand up for his ideas with his peers," because it helped him gain self-confidence. She designed classroom activities for students to develop and explain their opinions and to respectfully listen to the opinions of others. For example, Karen worked to create a trusting relationship with Armando, so he would take responsibility for his learning:

> Armando came up to me and he said, "Mrs. B, can you recommend a good cookbook? I want to check some cookbooks out of the library, because over spring break I want to do some cooking."
>
> I said, "Let's go look, and let me see if the library has them. If not, I'll bring you one that I have at home." For him to be able to ask that and talk about it, that's building that relationship.

Over the course of the year, Armando gained confidence. The relationship between Karen and Armando involved daily interchanges that eventually contributed to changing Armando's confidence level. Whether or not his attempts at independence were successful, after each attempt, he would try again. With each successful attempt, he grew more confident. He appeared happier as the year went on, because the independent behavior built his self-esteem.

Teach Students to Think for Themselves

Teaching students to think for themselves prepares them to be actively involved as responsible, democratic citizens. Independent thinking can be fostered in various grade-appropriate ways. Students need to be provided opportunities to explain, debate, and justify their thinking. Ann demonstrated to her second-grade students how a math problem could have more than one correct answer. She then gave her students the opportunity to explore the problem and compare their different approaches to it. Meera conducted student surveys in her fifth-grade class about their learning styles and collected a range of different answers, which she shared with them, promoting a discussion in which they compared their differences. She also used a classroom debate to teach about different perspectives:

> We had a debate about independence during the Revolutionary War, and that was interesting. All the students that got to be the Royalists were not happy, because they thought the Patriots would have more to say. But we talked about it, and I sat with the Loyalist group and said "I know you are at a disadvantage, but let's look at why you would want to be a Loyalist."

She set some parameters around the process. I told them "No name-calling; it will be a debate and you will have to listen to each other." Meera explained to her students the value of adopting a perspective that may be different from their own, and how doing so would ultimately help the students learn to formulate their opinions better:

> One Loyalist said, "You just don't want to pay the money. And the British came and helped; now when the British said you will have to pay for the soldiers, you are opposed to taxing." The debate was interesting; it really went well. They had to listen to what was said, because they had to formulate a response.

A sense of autonomy and the capacity to think for themselves also helps students make sense of the world, even the harsher realities as they become aware of inequities and stereotypes. As students build their capacity to self-reflect, they will eventually be able to analyze history and pervasive stereotypes and learn how to approach inequities in their own social environments.

CHALLENGES AND DILEMMAS

Teachers grapple with balancing an appropriate level of autonomy with supporting and sustaining students as they become more autonomous. We will explore three aspects of this challenge:

1. How much autonomy is enough?

2. How can we sustain students' efforts to act autonomously?

3. How can we ensure that students can manage themselves with their newfound autonomy?

How Much Autonomy Is Enough?

One challenge with increasing the level of autonomy involves providing the correct level of academic support—not too much nor too little help. In several of the classrooms at Karen's school, educational support professionals (ESPs) were assigned to particular special education students. These paraeducators, who were vital supports to the success of these students, sought to find alternatives to hovering over their assigned students, who were slower and more distracted than the others. Their role was to help with assigned work, but at the same time, they did not want to give the students a sense that they needed constant help. The ESPs feared that too much help would serve as a nonverbal message to students that they were not competent. The ESPs met with classroom teachers to find other ways to support students without offering help too soon.

Together, they came up with the following ways to approach this dilemma: The special education students were each given a behavior chart they could use themselves to monitor their completion of work. ESPs taught minilessons to particular students and then moved away to allow them to do increasing levels of independent work. To scaffold autonomy, Karen added peer support to ensure that the students were clear on assignments. Providing the opportunity for peer support is one way that classrooms that do not have adult support staff can help students who need extra help in learning.

How to Sustain Students' Efforts to Act Autonomously

Teachers face the dilemma of setting limits for classroom behavior while also allowing student autonomy. This autonomy helps students learn that, every single day, their life consists of making choices, and every choice has its consequence. If a teacher sets limits in a controlling manner, for example, "Do it because I said so," the students learn only to comply (or not) with the teacher's request. When the students understand the purpose of the limits and can participate in making choices within the limits, their autonomy is not undermined.

In an identity safe classroom, the teacher makes a conscious effort to give choices within the least restrictive environment. Students come to see themselves as having agency and being capable of autonomous behaviors when they sense that the teacher is aligned with them and in support of them. When the teacher sets the limits, he considers the following: Is it reasonable? Is it respectful? Do the students understand the reason for the limits? Do they know the consequences of not staying within the agreed-upon limits?

In one study, researchers wanted to examine differences in how young students respond to limits set in a supportive as opposed to a controlling style. They arranged for two groups of students to paint pictures. The teacher told the first group, "Be good boys and girls, don't make a mess, and don't mix up the colors." The teacher told the second group that she knew kids had fun slopping paint around, yet they "need to keep the painting area nice so that other students could paint too." The researchers found dramatic difference in results between the two groups. The second group, which was given "supported autonomy," was more enthusiastic, and the encouraging language had a "liberating" effect on them. Researchers surmised that the first group felt more manipulated and controlled, while the second group felt supported. The researchers felt that the study showed how to encourage and support students in taking responsibility for their behavior in an authentic way (Deci & Flaste, 1996).

Ensure Students Can Manage Themselves With Their Newfound Autonomy

The balance of authority and autonomy needs to be carefully determined in each classroom. At first it is hard to be supportive while setting limits, but teachers can learn to change how they speak to children, letting them know the reasons for these limits. A teacher might find herself feeling controlled by students who are well versed in manipulation. These students may take a teacher's offer of having a voice in decisions as a chance for negotiating. The process of finding a balance is a delicate dance of trial and error.

Sometimes we learn the most from our gravest errors. As a principal, Becki had a student, 11-year-old Willie, who was struggling with the ability to control his emotions and his tendencies to be a bully and act rudely in class, utterly defying his teachers. To make matters worse, he was a charismatic boy, and his peers both admired and feared him. He once confided to Becki that each night he prayed to act right in class. However, his difficulty controlling his impulses, together with the allure of having the whole class of fifth graders as an admiring audience, caused him to forget his best intentions.

On one occasion, Willie's teacher was absent. Becki took him to the library to work with a high school volunteer. She told the volunteer that since Willie often did not do well with substitutes, it would be best for him to work with this tutor in the library. Willie spent a good hour doing his work quietly and then begged to return to the classroom. Both he and the tutor promised Becki that he would work effectively in the classroom, and if he disrupted in any way, he would return to the library with the tutor, the minute the teacher told him to do so. Unfortunately, in the business of the day, Becki did not get to discuss the plan with his substitute.

The first several hours went very well. Later however, the whole class started becoming unruly, and things suddenly escalated for Willie. He was making funny noises and stood up on the table. The substitute, in an act she regretted terribly afterwards, grabbed onto Willie's sleeve to move him toward his seat. In a sudden impulse, Willie blew up, throwing himself over his desk and ultimately punching the filing cabinet, breaking his hand. Becki felt terrible, because she knew that in spite of Willie's best intentions to behave correctly with the substitute, he did not have the self-control to decide for himself when to return to the classroom.

PUTTING CLASSROOM AUTONOMY INTO PRACTICE

1. Think about what autonomy meant for you growing up.
   - Were you raised with a value of rugged individualism or a more collaborative view of success?

   - Were you given autonomy within the limits of your family's values?

2. Now, think about autonomy from your students' points of view.
   - What might autonomy look like in the families of your students?

   - What kind of freedoms do your students' families afford them?

(Continued)

(Continued)

- Are they allowed to play outside and move independently through the neighborhood?

- Are they allowed to stay over at friends' houses?

- Do some of your students come from families who value children having a sense of autonomy that is more or less than the school wants to promote?

- How might that affect their ability to acquire a more autonomous approach in the classroom?

Part II Summary

Child-centered teaching is a way of structuring a classroom rooted in child development theories focused on the social nature of learning. It is based on considering every aspect of the classroom from the point of view of each of the students to foster a sense of identity safety in them. In child-centered classrooms, teachers use many strategies to include students' perspectives, knowledge, experiences, and energy as tools for teaching and learning. This approach leads students to discover that who they are and what they can do matter.

To create an effective identity safe classroom, teachers do not leave student experiences to chance; every aspect of teaching is intentionally crafted to ensure each student's sense of belonging and full participation in the daily life of the classroom. Teachers construct the classroom environment based on students' needs, which are influenced by their backgrounds and prior knowledge.

Considering what students need can be a complicated process, where teachers may experience tension between trying not to be colorblind and not stereotyping. On the one hand we can say, "I treat everyone the same," but we may find that we're not really doing that, or that doing so does not actually meet the needs of a particular student. On the other hand, we do not want to use commonly held views of various cultures as the bases for our relationships with students. Our assumptions about what students need are, of course, influenced by our own experiences and assumptions that come from these experiences. For example, it is sometimes said that low-income children need more discipline than middle-class students, or that African American boys are more active than other boys. But, there is no supporting evidence for this.

Try to avoid such unintended stereotyping by reflecting on your assumptions and checking in with students directly. Talking directly with students to learn what they need or think is a good way to avoid being colorblind. Our students are our best teachers. We can check our assumptions about the basis of a problem by actually talking with students. They will learn from these interactions that you have their best interests in mind, even if you cannot fully meet their needs or agree with them every time.

Teachers also consider the social and academic expectations and societal stereotypes that influence students' sense of themselves as successful students. Teachers tailor the environment to the particular students in the classroom, helping develop a sense of self by listening to the expression of their ideas and beliefs (student voice); teaching so that students' understand and connect what they have learned with what they know (teaching for understanding); focusing on cooperation rather than competition in their relationships with one another (cooperation); and finally, fostering increasing levels of independence and responsibility (autonomy).

These four factors of child-centered teaching are interrelated, but thinking about them individually will help remind teachers of various approaches to use. By seeking out students' ideas and feelings, teachers can learn about their students and use what the students know to build students' knowledge in the classroom. But, there are challenges and dilemmas associated with incorporating these four factors into the classroom:

- Teachers are faced with the challenge of Listening for Student Voices without fostering a sense of entitlement or loss of focus in the classroom.
- Teaching for Understanding requires teachers to determine that each student deeply understands a lesson before moving on to new learning objectives. For students who have not achieved that deep understanding, teachers may have to try strategies such as reteaching or providing peer support to ensure that all the students are ready for a new lesson.
- Focus on Cooperation emphasizes the social context for learning by explicitly teaching students ways to work together and care for one another. Because competition is often more highly valued by parents, students, and other teachers, students may have had little or no practice with cooperative relationships. They may need much support at the beginning to believe in and practice this approach.
- Teachers are faced with finding a balance of structure and freedom. They may find it challenging to give sufficient support and scaffolding for Classroom Autonomy while still providing increasing levels of independence. Promoting autonomy becomes further complicated by students with special needs who have difficulty working independently and taking responsibility for their actions.

In identity safe classrooms, child-centered teaching practices ensure that students understand and can explain what they are learning and have opportunities for exploration and curiosity to flourish. This approach will begin to help students learn to analyze their lives critically, make decisions for themselves, and take responsibility for their thoughts and actions as they work cooperatively with others. This level of engagement contributes to a sense of confidence and safety, as students gain a sense of ownership for their actions, learn to work together to become creative problem solvers, and are empowered to act responsibly in concert with a range of diverse individuals and groups in the world.

Part II References

Barkley, R. (2005). *ADHD and the nature of self-control.* New York, NY: Guilford Press.

Boaler, J., & Staples, M. (2008). Creating mathematical futures through an equitable teaching approach: The case of Railside School. *The Teachers College Record, 110*(3), 608–645.

Child Development Project. (1996). *Ways we want our class to be: Class meetings that build commitment to kindness and learning.* Oakland, CA: Developmental Studies Center.

Child Development Project. (1997). *Blueprints for a collaborative classroom.* Oakland, CA: Developmental Studies Center.

Costa, A. (2008). *The school as a home for the mind: Creating mindful curriculum, instruction, and dialogue.* Thousand Oaks, CA: Corwin.

Darling-Hammond, L. (2010). *The flat world and education: How America's commitment to equity will determine our future.* New York, NY: Teachers College Press.

Deci, E., & Flaste, R. (1996). *Why we do what we do: Understanding self-motivation.* New York, NY: Penguin Books.

Deci, E., & Ryan, R. (1985). *Intrinsic motivation and self-determination in human behavior.* New York: Plenum Press.

Glenn, H. S., & Nelsen, J. (1989). *Raising self-reliant children in a self-indulgent world.* Rocklin, CA: Prima.

Greene, R. (2008). *Lost at school: Why our kids with behavioral challenges are falling through the cracks and how we can help them.* New York, NY: Simon & Schuster.

Levine, M. (2006). *The price of privilege: How parental pressure and material advantage are creating a generation of disconnected and unhappy kids.* New York, NY: Harper and Collins.

Marzano, R. J. (1998). *A theory-based meta-analysis of research in instruction* (Tech. Rep.). Aurora, CO: Mid-continent Regional Educational Laboratory (ERIC Document Reproduction Service No. ED 427 087).

Mayhew, K. C., & Edwards, A. C. (1936). *The Dewey School.* New York: Appleton-Century.

Meisels, S. J., Marsden, D. B., Jablon, J. R., Dorfman, A. B., & Dichtelmiller, M. K. (1998). *The Work sampling system.* San Antonio, TX: Pearson.

Sousa, D. (2006). *How the brain learns.* Thousand Oaks, CA: Corwin.

Steele, D. M. (2012). Identity-safe school environments, creating. In J. A. Banks (Ed.), *Encyclopedia of diversity in education* (Vol. 1, pp. 1125–1128). Thousand Oaks, CA: Sage.

Sylwester, R. (2007). *The adolescent brain: Reaching for autonomy.* Thousand Oaks, CA: Corwin.

Part III

Cultivating Diversity as a Resource

WHAT DO WE MEAN BY CULTIVATING DIVERSITY AS A RESOURCE?

The diversity in language, culture, skill levels, and personal experience with school life that students bring to classrooms is often thought of as a problem rather than a resource. Yet, classrooms cannot really be identity safe without embracing the differences in the classroom as resources for learning (Steele, D. M., 2012). And, dealing with diverse students is a complicated and nuanced process. When teachers do not feel confident about what to do, they often resort to strategies that can be ineffective and even, unintentionally, instantiate stereotypes and a sense that "difference is unimportant," or that difference means "deficiency."

When teachers limit their diversity efforts to pictures on the wall, an occasional assembly, or the celebration of food and cultures in a way that does not truly engage students in learning about one another, their students miss opportunities to feel valued and to gain respect and curiosity not only about their different histories, languages, cultures, and perspectives but also about their own identities.

Teachers may also feel that with all the pressures on the school day to meet a long list of standards, raise test scores, maintain records, and deal with individual student problems, they do not have time to "do diversity." Yet, our students live in an increasingly diverse world and one that is ever more globalized. One of the most important things for them to learn is that there are many perspectives, understandings, and ways of doing things. The process of learning to reconcile these differences and include new ideas into their own thinking and assumptive world is essential for their success in school and later. Reducing learning to the particular facts at hand will not provide them with the resources they need to live as adults in a democratic society.

The deficit thinking described above is the view that the students of color are somehow "lacking" and must be educated "in spite of" their backgrounds. In addition many teachers fail to recognize the need to move away from colorblind practices. This approach, a deficit model paired with colorblind practices, leads to a devastating result across the nation—a growing school-to-prison pipeline. This pipeline begins in elementary school, where African American and Latino students are referred to special education, suspended, and expelled at rates higher than their white and Asian peers (Drakeford, 2006).

The fundamental reason for encouraging the intentional practice of continuously looking at the classroom through a lens of diversity is that, without this effort, students from diverse backgrounds cannot have a psychological sense of actually belonging as valued members of the class. Our research showed us that doing diversity is much more than celebrating difference. Doing diversity well is not an add-on but is central to the way that we do everything in the classroom. We learned from our Stanford Integrated Schools Project (SISP) research that there are three essential aspects of doing diversity: Using Diversity as a Resource for Teaching, High Expectations and Academic Rigor, and a Challenging Curriculum. Here are short definitions of these three factors of cultivating diversity in the classroom.

Using Diversity as a Resource for Teaching involves drawing on the students' backgrounds in both the process and content of teaching every day and giving genuine value to their experiences and points of view. Effective strategies include many that educators often think of when considering how to teach in diverse classrooms. These include grouping students in diverse working groups; displaying books, art, and music from different backgrounds; mentioning important contributions of individuals of all ethnic backgrounds; using world languages in the class; and asking students to include their own experiences and histories in their work. An important aspect of this approach is that diversity is a part of daily life and not saved for special holiday events.

Helping all students develop academic and social competence, as well as an awareness of their own competence, is the purpose of Using Diversity as a Resource for Teaching in identity safe classrooms. The *Oxford English Dictionary* defines competence as "the ability to do something successfully or effectively." According to Andrew J. Elliot and Carol Dweck (2005), competence is considered to be an inherent human need and an underlying motivating force across a person's lifespan; it is ubiquitous in all aspects of human life and across all cultures. Josh Aronson and Claude Steele (2005) point out that a student's sense of competence can be fragile but also can be responsive to intervention. Intellectual competence is influenced not only by capacity but also is a result of both real experiences and perceptions that result from interactions with others. Unless we look deeper, both the student and the teacher may assume that low grades or test scores are the product of internal assets like a lack of giftedness while ignoring the influence of powerful situational factors and social climate. As described in Chapter 1 of this book, stereotype threat has been found to have a profound influence on academic achievement and competence. In this chapter, we explore ways to shift the social climate through high expectations for student success in the context of challenging and rigorous curriculum while drawing on student diversity as a resource for learning. We examine ways to do this through communicating these expectations together with scaffolding and differentiating instruction to meet a variety of needs.

High Expectations and Academic Rigor are reflected in teachers' expectations for student learning, which are expressed in many different ways throughout the day (Steele, D. M., 2012). Dealing with students' differences in academic background and skill levels is one of the most challenging tasks for teachers. Yet, this may be the nexus of the problem of teaching all students an academically rigorous curriculum. When students are regularly pulled out of class for tutoring or given less meaningful, rote-learning tasks, they can feel like second-class citizens in the classroom, and their attachment to learning will be reduced. In this chapter we will show how teachers can express high expectations through academic rigor by creating open-ended learning tasks focused on high levels of thinking. We will show ways to scaffold students' learning to move them toward mastery and to focus all the students on becoming prepared to go to college.

A Challenging Curriculum creates an air of intellectual excitement and occurs when teachers ask students for inference, hypothesis, and deduction. It is essential that teachers use curricula, materials, and learning tasks that have meaning for all of their students, and that it includes experiences, images, and references from the many cultures and lived experiences of the students.

In these next three chapters, we will explain why each of the identity safety factors of Cultivating Diversity as a Resource is important and give examples of how to put them into practice. We recognize that diversity is a complex topic, made even more difficult because student identities are constantly changing as they develop and interact in a classroom. We will draw from relevant research and highlight some of the challenges. While each situation is unique, we will share how educators have addressed the process of cultivating diversity as a resource in several different classrooms with varied demographics.

Using Diversity as a Resource for Teaching

WHY USE DIVERSITY AS A RESOURCE FOR TEACHING?

Our focus on Diversity as a Resource for Teaching is in direct contrast to a colorblind approach to teaching. The concept of diversity as a resource applies to all types of differences (e.g., race, gender, class, sexual orientation, and disabilities). Though our focus has been on those social identities (race, ethnicity, and class) that have been historically associated with negative stereotypes about the academic abilities of students from those groups, when teachers make efforts to create a safe classrooms for any of the students, it can become a safer place for *all* the children. That is, the process of thinking about the classroom from the perspective of one group of students can lead to thinking about all the students. Teachers exemplify their attitudes about diversity and difference in everything they say and do in the classroom. When teachers ignore differences that are linked to negative stereotypes in school, it does not make the differences invisible to the members of the class, especially not those students whose social identities are being ignored.

We begin with the assumption that teachers do not intend to stereotype students. Teachers often strive to be colorblind so they will not inadvertently act in a racist manner. We also know that none of us is an expert in *all* the histories, languages, and cultural interpretations that children bring with them to school. And, importantly, this focus is based on the premise that teaching and learning is a complex social-psychological process and that it matters profoundly to who we are and how we relate to one another in the classroom (Markus, Steele, C. M., & Steele, D. M., 2000).

The focus of this resource approach to diversity is to consider carefully every aspect of the classroom from the perspectives of the students in the class. This approach is not about simply avoiding overt racism or stereotyping, but about creating an inclusive, curious, dynamic, academically rigorous environment in the classroom. It is also important to teach students how to work together, to show interest in and respect for one another, and to work toward creating a safe, strong environment for learning. We learned from the SISP study that diversity as a resource is manifested through teachers including all students in complex levels of learning, using student names correctly, validating students' languages by asking them to use words from their home language, and incorporating culturally relevant materials and teaching practices across the day and school year. It is also important to recognize that some students have multiple ethnic identities that teachers may not observe. In fact, we all have multiple social identities, including race, gender, and religion, that form different aspects of who we are. In different situations, different aspects of our identities are salient.

This chapter describes many avenues for approaching diversity as a resource. We give examples for using culture as content in the classroom, both formally and informally, by drawing from the students' backgrounds in natural ways through music, literature, language, and current events. We show that teachers can help create a feeling of unity in the classroom, so students can practice positive, caring relationships with one another and not fear that their group membership is a barrier to school success. We also examine ways to use critical multiculturalism as a tool to help students analyze negative and stereotypical messages in school and in the world. This ability to analyze is crucial when students learn about the history of intergroup relationships in the United States and when stereotypes or conflicts enter the daily life of the classroom. Then we look at ways to reduce prejudice and stereotyping and to equalize status in the classroom.

Finally, we move to looking at some dilemmas that may arise when addressing diversity as a resource in diverse classrooms. Throughout the chapter, we show teachers helping students develop a positive identity leading to a healthy view of self with a sense of purpose, hope in the future, and personal efficacy. The examples we give are simple and do not require extensive lesson planning. We found through our SISP research that these regular, ongoing, validating experiences, taken together with the other factors, lead students to do better on state-mandated standardized tests, to feel identity safe, and to like school more than students in colorblind classrooms.

Building on Important Research in Multicultural Education and Intergroup Relations

The research on stereotype threat and identity safety is the foundation of our work, but we also draw from the work of other leaders in education and the field of social psychology whose research has influenced educators seeking to create equitable outcomes in diverse classrooms.

For example, one body of research that influences our thinking on *how* to use diversity as a resource comes from the work of social psychologists whose research has been dedicated to exploring ways to reduce prejudice in group settings. Much of this recent work is based on the earlier work of Gordon Allport (1954), whose notion of how to reduce prejudice was called the *contact hypothesis.* This important early work showed that prejudice can be reduced only when people have the chance to know one another and learn to see similarities as well as differences between them. The contact hypothesis provides a conceptual tool for teachers to use to create less prejudiced, more inclusive groups of students.

Following on Allport's early work, more recent work by psychologists provides the basis for understanding some of the processes involved in creating successful contact among diverse students. We will show how creating equal status and promoting cooperative interdependence among students, and creating opportunities for students to learn new information about their classmates' cultural and historic backgrounds, will benefit all the students.

James Banks and Cherry Banks (2003) have been leading researchers in multicultural education for the last four decades. They define *content integration* as curriculum that incorporates perspectives from a variety of cultures, including pride in one's own heritage, appreciation of other cultures, knowledge of historical contributions, and understanding of the influence of power and privilege on all ethnicities. They propose that teachers analyze frames of reference, perspectives, and biases that influence ways in which knowledge is constructed and help students delve into the content through questioning, exploration, and critical inquiry.

Banks and Banks use the concept of *equity pedagogy* to describe an approach that addresses the diverse learning styles of students from differing backgrounds. They remind teachers to focus on inclusive practices rather than cultural stereotypes while exposing students to standards of the dominant society to prepare them for success in the world. Banks and Banks highlight the need to go beyond curriculum content alone to cultivate diversity as a resource in all our teaching practices and school structures. (See Allport, 1954; Banks & Banks, 2003; Dovidio & Gaertner,

2000; and Pettigrew & Tropp, 2005, for a more thorough discussion of these concepts and their theoretical underpinnings.)

USING DIVERSITY AS A RESOURCE FOR TEACHING: HOW TO DO IT

Cultivate an Equity Lens

Identity safety teaching practices are based on teachers' attention to the way that each student is affected by what is going on in the classroom. Throughout each day, teachers can ask themselves, "How is this lesson or assignment or activity being experienced by each student?" It is obvious that a teacher cannot look at each of her students every time she asks herself this question, but by considering two or three different students at a time, soon she will come to be more aware of how all her students are experiencing the class.

A central question for teachers to consider is how to equalize status in the classroom. This is a difficult, but important, aspect of eliminating stereotype threat and creating identity safety. Ongoing efforts to create equal status are necessary for the reduction of prejudice. Many teachers address diversity only with what is known as the "tourist" curriculum, which reduces multiculturalism to a superficial tour through various cultures via holidays. It is hard for teachers to avoid thinking about traditional holidays in ways that may actually instantiate stereotypes (Lee, Menkart, & Okazawa-Rey, 1998). For example, Becki commented, "More than one African American parent has pointed out to me how year after year their children study Dr. Martin Luther King's 'I have a Dream' speech, asking why teachers can't go beyond it to the rich traditions of African American literature."

A sense of equity is created when teachers intentionally help students explore shared and different histories, languages, and perspectives throughout the year and across the curriculum. Students flourish when they see themselves and the groups they belong to reflected on a daily basis, and so they are not seen as an "other."

Ann described ways she incorporated diverse histories to teach geography to her second grade students:

> I have a beautiful set of photos of children around the world on the wall. They are arranged by continent, and each one has the name of a country posted underneath it. I use these along with books about different cultures. I have a collection of ABC books from countries around the world. I use these books for our first

major project, the *ABC's of Me*, where the students write about their relationships, heritage and culture, physical characteristics, personality, interests, hobbies, and favorites. We also display [where their families are from] on a world map.

In addition, by having an "equity lens," Ann was able to take advantage of teachable moments:

> Daniel, who did not speak English, is a very social kid, with no trouble communicating even in Mandarin to everyone. One day he made everyone folded paper boxes. That afternoon, I got out scrap paper and he taught all the students how to make boxes, something that was part of his Chinese culture.

Having an equity lens means that teachers are on the alert for situations that might affect learning, such as celebration of a holiday in a manner that is not inclusive of all students. With an eye to equity, teachers pay attention to subtle messages like ensuring that crayons or supplies labeled as "flesh" are the color of students' skins. They explicitly value the use of primary languages and find ways to bring them into daily classroom life. They express genuine interest in where students' families come from, including specific countries in Africa, Asia, or Latin America or even different parts of the United States. They highlight the value of biculturalism as opposed to one-way assimilation and consider the unique challenges faced by biracial and multiethnic students who might not feel totally accepted by either group. These examples show that continually incorporating simple activities into the curriculum is more powerful than major cultural events that highlight differences as "otherness."

An equity lens also allows teachers to notice other kinds of difference that may not be as easy to see, like students with gay parents. Teachers can find ways to acknowledge many realities and differences in positive ways so that students do not feel singled out. Writing activities or opportunities to reflect on and to share from their personal lives give students the chance to connect with their backgrounds in a positive way that lets them be in control of the information that is disclosed. Reading literature that incorporates a wide range of issues and topics can signal support for students who have these differences and can serve as a teaching tool for the others.

Once students feel safe, discussions and activities that invite them to express their own thoughts and perspectives can lead to students thinking about and sharing how their social identities influence their experiences. Simple comments from teachers that show they are unbiased and do not tolerate teasing and prejudice go a long way to model acceptance in the class.

Julia reported,

When I was teaching fourth grade, I found that even in a classroom with all Latino students, differences in social status were present depending on how much English the child spoke or whether the child was born in the United States or Mexico. I found it difficult to alter the natural tendency of students to compare themselves to and compete with their peers, so I designed a game where students lined up based on where they were born in relationship to Oakland, where they attended school. Everyone got excited as they used a globe to discover that New York was actually farther away from Oakland than Tijuana. It was a good way to experience that they all had equal value no matter where they were born. Then the children wrote stories about where they were born.

Create an Environment of Acceptance and Equal Status

The complex process of creating an environment of acceptance can even mean changing the routine of the entire class to meet the needs of a particular student. Meera was aware of Andy's need to shift his image of himself to help him build relationships with his classmates:

Andy came to my class with a chip on his shoulder. He is the only African American boy in the entire fifth grade. He had moved to our school in third grade and was never really accepted by the other students. Academically, his performance was low, and he went to the literacy summer [intervention] program in third and fourth grade. By doing my interest inventory and surveys, I discovered he was really smart and where he needed the extra support and confidence.

I worked with him all year, giving him the benefit of the doubt and trusting him. Building that trust with him was the foundation of all learning that happened this year. Not only did I gain his trust, but also by having courageous conversations about race and diversity in the class, I was able to make the other kids see what a neat child Andy was. Andy learned to play and work together with all students. Students in my class stand up for him on the playground. He feels that he belongs.

To create a classroom environment of acceptance, teachers need to help build trust and a sense of mutual caring in the classroom. This effort is particularly important in racially and economically diverse classrooms, especially when student academic achievement levels are associated with students' group identities. In a class where African American or Latino students are the minority, the risk of stereotype threat about their academic success is greater than in homogeneous classrooms.

For example, Ann drew on a nonacademic success to leverage status and acceptance for Rob:

> Rob has learning disabilities that are making him stand out more and more in the class. He is becoming self-conscious as he realizes that he is different and that he can't do everything the other students can do. I found out that his favorite song is "Johnny Be Good" and that he and his brother imitate Chuck Berry and the band performing the song. I asked Rob if he would like to teach the class that song. He had to plan the lesson with his aide and ask another teacher for the words (she wrote them on easel paper). His father made a video of the boys performing. Rob did a good job "teaching," and the students loved the video. The whole class will start singing the refrain at times. Encouraging Rob to do this boosted his confidence and status in the class. Now all the students see him differently.

Rob's acceptance and subsequent elevated social status as a result of his musical performance enhanced his liking of school and eventually his connection with his classmates, which allowed him to feel safe to take risks in the academic arena. In an identity safe classroom, teachers find many pathways to spark interest and increase motivation to learn and achieve social and academic competence.

Encourage Cooperative Interdependence

When the IDS study group (author Becki Cohn-Vargas's identity safety study group) studied about the common in-group identity theory (Dovidio & Gaertner, 2000), they realized that much of what they did in their classrooms to create a sense of identity safety incorporated the notion called *decategorization*. This process shifts the focus on separate identities toward commonalities as individuals get to know one another. Students in their classrooms had lots of personal contact that helped them learn to appreciate each other as individuals without focusing on their differences. Yet, the teachers also recognized that decategorization alone is not enough and can actually be the basis for colorblind teaching practices.

Instead, the teachers learned that the theory described by Dovidio and Gaertner (2000) went further. It included *recategorization* within the dual identity model that the researchers considered the most promising strategy for reducing prejudice and bringing diverse groups of people together. This dual identity model forms the basis of a noncolorblind, identity safe classroom, in which student subgroup identities are validated in the context of cooperative interdependence. In identity safe classrooms, students work together in cooperative groups for a shared goal, yet their individual and group identities (e.g., African American, Latino, Egyptian, and Israeli) can remain salient and valued. The dual identity model best promotes equal status in the classroom, because students feel they are validated for who they are—they feel more identity safe.

Julia highlighted different students' contributions in a safe and structured way. She used cooperative learning groups to teach her fifth grade students skills for working together, often changing leadership roles and group membership. She took time to point out unique qualities the different students brought to their roles. For example, she said, "Keisha is a good organizer who is able to make a list of the tasks needed to help her group finish the project." She pointed out how Miguel taught the others some sayings he learned from his grandmother in El Salvador that made their newspaper more interesting.

Maintaining the value of cooperative interdependence needs constant revisiting in the classroom, including when resolving incidents that take place on the schoolyard. Dorothy gave an example from her son's experience and in a fourth–sixth grade combination classroom:

> All the boys wanted to play football during recess, but the older boys tended to be more successful in claiming the use of the football, leaving the fourth grade boys, like my son Benny, out of the game. This exclusion, of course, made Benny angry. He thought the whole setup was unfair. Benny's teacher knew that having such a mix of grade levels in her classroom created an imbalance of power; however, she had her hands full with this blended classroom. So her solution was to make the rule that once the students crossed the threshold of the classroom door after recess, no more discussion of playground events was allowed. Unfortunately for Benny, the consequence of continuing the playground conversation was to be "awarded" minutes, which meant he could not even go to the playground after a certain number of minutes were accumulated.

But these kids needed help. If the teacher had stopped to talk with the students to help them find another way to handle this conflict, they would have learned something about how to cooperate for everyone's benefit, and the teacher would have to have been less dependent on her discipline tactic of keeping young boys off the playground when they needed to practice playing together and to get some exercise!

Help Students Get to Know One Another

One of the best ways to reduce stereotypes and prejudice is getting to know a person as an individual. One of the simplest strategies for teachers to foster mutual understanding is through grouping students. Becki shared,

> I always shifted my groups to assure that all my students got a chance to work with everyone. They got to work with partners, sit in table groups, and engage in cooperative activities with each of the other students. I also took opportunities for my students to meet others outside their classrooms by having buddy classes that paired them with students in a different grade level. This gave them a chance to really get to know students from other backgrounds in a safe and supported way. This is one of the best ways to promote intercultural friendships and understanding.

Holding class meetings is another strategy teachers can use to enhance students' knowledge of one another. When held regularly, class meetings help students really learn about one another and see one another's strengths and interests. Class meetings can be held at the beginning or end of each day to either plan the day or to review how things went. Meetings can be focused on topics of interest linked to the curriculum in which students can see the knowledge and skill held by some students that have not been obvious to the class previously. Teachers may also use these meetings to encourage students to help solve problems in the classroom. For example, if students are having difficulties managing their use of computers, the teacher can engage them in finding a solution that allows all students to have access to the computers. This process will help the students identify with and carry out the new strategy for sharing. Though these meetings take some time, the benefit to students for creating a sense of belonging and community are priceless. This may lead to better helping behavior and cooperation, an enhanced ability to focus on learning, and a stronger sense of belonging for all students.

Expose Students to New Cultural Knowledge

Unfortunately, the tourist curriculum described earlier can actually reinforce stereotypes. The curriculum needs to extend beyond those stereotypical images and embrace cultures represented in the classroom by weaving images and references from lived experiences into the daily life of the classroom. Simple activities can be done regularly and integrated right into the standards of the grade level.

For example, in the IDS study group we talked about how literature provides an entry point for talking about all kinds of differences and creates possibilities for open-ended discussions about race and culture. A rich array of multicultural literature is available, but it is up to teachers to help students link the literature to their lives. This literature can include folk tales, real-life stories, biographies, and expository texts that highlight contributions made by people from all cultures represented in the classroom. One example is an assignment entitled "a scientist like me" where students research scientists of their ethnic or cultural backgrounds.

In another example, Ken (Grade 4) described "cultural boxes" as an activity he does yearly to expose his students to new cultures and practices:

> We do cultural boxes in the beginning of the year. Students each make an "apartment" using a 12-inch by 12-inch three-dimensional box. They do drawings and bring things from home to put in their apartments. They can share any special family celebration. We see all of these people in the boxes are celebrating family traditions. When we put the boxes up on the wall, each one is like an apartment in a building. The project also includes a piece of writing to describe the cultural box.

Another simple, yet powerful, way to promote knowledge of language and cultural practices is to ask students to share what they know with other students. During an English grammar lesson, a Chinese student lit up when Ken asked her to show the class how Mandarin is based on intonations. She smiled and shared a tongue twister in Mandarin. Learning about the Mandarin language helped give students a new appreciation for the differences in how languages work to the English speakers in his classroom.

These types of activities take minimal preparation time and yield many positive returns. Students love to share coins, games, food items, family celebrations, and toys that reflect their cultural backgrounds. Bringing parents into the classroom to read to students in their primary language, to read to the class and have their child translate into English, to share photos and stories from their families, or to describe the work they do introduces all the students to the parents' knowledge and know-how and can create a strong sense of pride for the child of these visiting parents. Visits from family members and other role models are extremely helpful, especially when the students do not have teachers from their own ethnic groups. Ann tried to invite every parent who was willing to come to her second grade classroom. This invitation served as a source of pride to both the child and the parent.

Karen wanted her fifth grade students to meet successful people from their racial/ethnic backgrounds. She invited one of her professors to speak to her class:

> The professor brought toys she played with as a little girl, and she told about all of her experiences from Mexico. As soon as the professor came in, Elena [a student in the class] looked at me and was glowing; she was front and center. And she recognized a lot of the toys. Now I realize that I need to go out into the community and find more people who are willing to come in.

Ken had a stream of college students come to his fourth grade classroom, because, as young people, their stories of how they got to college could motivate his students. The IDS study group members agreed that seeing a person who represented their ethnic background helps to build confidence in the students of color. But something else important happens. Having successful visitors from different backgrounds confirms for white students, too, that people from many backgrounds make important contributions to our society.

Address the Hard Conversations About Race and Culture in Curriculum

At home, students are exposed to television that depicts stereotypical views of different racial groups and often profiles people of color as criminals. To give students tools to deconstruct the myths and counteract negative images, Karen and Meera brought news items, magazines, and movies to class as alternative sources of information on race and culture. They were cognizant that in spite of progress, history books still tell the story of the past from a dominant, or mainstream, perspective. To broaden their students' perspectives, they taught the students to critically analyze cultural examples found in the media and texts that reinforce negative stereotypes. This analysis, known as *critical multiculturalism,* is an approach that teaches students to understand racial situations. Students are taught to take a critical look at situations and current events through an equity lens in the context of historical inequities (Nieto, 1998).

Even very young children are able to participate in a critical analysis. Dorothy described her amazement when her second grade son was "required" to watch Saturday morning cartoons by his teacher.

The students' job was to look for gender and racial stereotyping in the cartoons. And her son, who was previously not supposed to watch TV on Saturday morning, was one happy analyst!

Starting in kindergarten, students are aware of race and stereotypes (Ambady, Shih, Kim, & Pitinsky, 2001). Determined to raise awareness of equity for her first grade students, Becki taught about the Montgomery bus boycott by having the students do a very simple play. They set up rows of chairs and took the parts of Rosa Parks, Martin Luther King, the bus driver, and community members, simply reenacting the story of how the right to sit anywhere on the bus was won. At the age of six, students easily understood how unfair it was to force African American people to sit in the back of the bus. These young students could appreciate how unjust these laws were because of their own very age-appropriate concern for fairness.

Karen used current news items to involve her fifth grade students in real conversations about race and discrimination:

> Armando never talked about his background. He had a quiet connection with his family's origins. He's very empathetic and tolerant of all cultures, very caring, and paid attention to detail with other kids. He needed more confidence with his self-image and the image of his culture. He didn't want to talk about it at first. He didn't want it to come up. At times we had multicultural activities with sharing and listening, and we had several difficult conversations based on student questions. Armando listened intently, although he didn't participate.
>
> Only after Elena, his classmate, repeatedly talked about her culture, did he bring in a current event item about immigration. This, in turn, motivated Elena to share a distressing news article about a noncommercial video game highlighting immigration. The person playing the game gets points for shooting Mexicans as they try to cross the border.

This distressing article, shared by a student, gave all the students in the class an opportunity to think about and discuss how such games affect others' sense of belonging and safety. Clearly, Elena felt safe enough to share something that could have made her feel vulnerable. Elena's teacher, Karen, described another conversation prompted by another article brought to class by Elena.

> Well, Elena brought a *Newsweek* article (with a picture captioned "Web of Hate, Scene From the Anti-Immigration Border Patrol"

[Reno, 2006]) and said "Look, Mrs. B.," and she wanted to share it with the class. She said, "This is the kind of video games they're coming up with, shooting the Mexicans when they come over the border."

Well, you know what Elena said after this? "California's one of the strongest states with the most money, and that is on the backs of my cousins. They work down in Modesto. And they work really hard, and they sometimes can't even go home to Mexico." She was heated about it.

Karen had a teachable moment that lead to a critical look at history and current racial discrimination. She provided a way for the children to understand the news items and to deal with the feelings of Elena and Armando and the other students as they learned about the harsh realities of racism.

News coverage about devastating hurricanes and floods brought up issues of race in Meera's fifth grade class. She asked her students to look critically and weigh the evidence:

Take something like New Orleans. Previously, we had a discussion about race, and just today when we saw there was flooding in New Hampshire; I asked, "Do you think the government is going to act the same way it acted in New Orleans?" One of my kids raised her hand and said, "No I don't think it is going to happen that way, the reason being in New Orleans there are a lot of African Americans and in New Hampshire, there are a lot of white people, so the government is going to act differently." Another student said, "They probably learned something from the New Orleans flood, and they are more prepared." And somebody else said, "New Orleans people must feel pretty unhappy because they didn't fix those levees."

Research on racial identity formation posits that as children grow up, they accumulate experiences that lead them to develop positive or negative racial and ethnic identities (Nieto, 1999; Tatum, 1997). A critical multicultural approach used in an age-appropriate way helps students from both nondominant and dominant groups to develop positive identities for themselves and genuine acceptance and appreciation of others. Students of color learn to combat stereotype threat and find their voice. All students, whether from dominant or other backgrounds, learn to deconstruct stereotypes and critique their own behavior and what they see around them. This empowerment has an equalizing effect on status for all the students.

Address and Intervene in Incidents of Stereotyping, Stereotype Threat, and Racism

It was good to have several grade levels represented in the IDS study group because the teachers came to realize that incidents involving stereotyping happen at every grade level. It is incumbent on us as teachers to use age-appropriate ways to respond to bias and stereotypes. Meera shared a turning point for her son at the age of four:

> I have to tell you about my son; his name is Siddhartha and it is a long name. All his young life, he had heard only the name Siddhartha. When he was in preschool, his teacher thought that name was too long. So, she called him Sid, and he didn't respond. So, his teacher said, "Might I call you Sid?" And he answered, "No, my name is Siddhartha; my name is not Sid." He was only four years old, and he wanted to be called Siddhartha. Since then all his friends have learned his name, and all his teachers have called him Siddhartha.

Another way to address stereotype threat is to approach it proactively, without singling out any of the students. Yesenia, one of Meera's students, experienced stereotype threat because she had been held back a grade:

> She's a year older than a typical fifth grader. She's 11, but what happened is she never wanted to tell her age. Her mom came to me at the beginning of the year saying that to whomever she met, she'd say that she was 10 years old. Her mom said, "I don't want her to feel like she's one of the older kids." I decided to do an activity in class that would get all the students to tell their ages without Yesenia feeling singled out. So, I asked them about their birthdays and asked how many were 11. She looked around and found that there were five kids older than she was.

In addition to unspoken stereotype threat, Meera heard overt racist comments and stereotypical attitudes expressed in her classroom. Meera taught her students about speaking up:

> When Andy came to our school, people immediately assumed that he was being bused like most of our other African American students. His dad is a neurosurgeon at the local university medical school, and he lives near our school. It was an assumption, and so we have had a lot of discussion about racism, and I think the kids do notice when it happens.

Actually, Andy brings it up very nicely, "My brother Will was on this tee ball team; it was a local team, and another boy says to his mother, 'Is that brown boy on our team?' My mom felt really bad, but she didn't say anything. I told my mom, you should speak up; that is what Mrs. O. said to do."

Intervening also requires teachers to address uncomfortable subjects that do not have simple answers. Meera (Grade 5) talked about one boy, Avi, an Israeli, who spoke of how he was worried about the missiles falling on his relatives. Another boy, Ahmed, was Egyptian, and he told Meera he had cousins in Lebanon, saying, "We haven't been able to talk to them." Meera says of these exchanges,

> It's really hard to bring those issues up in the classroom, but I understand that they're here. I told them, "Your parents are from there, but you're American; we're all Americans." I even said, "I come from India, but I'm an American, and yes, things that happen in our [ancestral] countries bother us."
>
> Recently Avi and Ahmed had a play date. It turned out both their moms spoke Arabic, and they realized they had much in common and traded recipes. So, lots of issues come up with all the different kids that we have. We talk about globalization and have people from around the globe, right in our classroom.

Karen helped her students deal with the emotions that result from examining racism and other of the world's many harsh realities. She explained to them "It's okay to be angry. But let's take a look at that anger and why it's happening. It's hard to do, but it's well worth the time." In identity safe classrooms, teachers need to be self-reflective about their own stereotypes and, through that understanding, allow for differing student opinions. Reflection is an ongoing process of examining one's own assumptions, beliefs, and attitudes. This practice, combined with the willingness to have often difficult, but usually powerful, conversations with students, will help them learn to question assumptions. These choices are not easy and require constant negotiation, judgment calls, and vigilance to avoid overreacting or making errors of omission.

Support Students With Two Same-Gender Parents

Many teachers feel anxious about discussing issues pertaining to LGBT (lesbian, gay, bisexual, and transgender) people. While "don't ask, don't tell" policies have been eliminated from the army, and laws protect against homophobic slurs and harassment, most schools, particularly elementary schools, still do not address these issues. In 2010, five gay teen suicides in a three-week period in the United States put a spotlight on homophobic bullying and harassment, which often starts in grade school. Schools continue to be very unsafe places for LGBT teachers and students as well as for children of LGBT parents. Bullying also impacts learning and achievement. LGBT teachers are often silenced by fear, and students do not even get the benefit of the many LGBT role models who are working in schools.

Becki reported,

> Individual teachers claim they are unsure of how to address these topics and worry that they will be perceived as promoting a gay lifestyle. In other cases, teachers and administrators have said that elementary school students are too young to discuss sex. I always answer that while the discussion of sex is included in specific parts of the curriculum, the discussion of safety is needed at all times for all students. I tell them that it is crucial that students know that homophobic comments are not acceptable, and that when teachers address this issue, students need to hear that there are different types of couples in the world, including two men and two women. All have a right to feel safe.

For the same reason that we believe colorblind practices are a barrier to students thriving in school, we believe that teachers cannot create identity safe classrooms without specifically including all students, including those who may be invisibly experiencing homophobia, whether they personally don't fit standard gender roles or whether they have LGBT family members.

Becki described,

> In my primarily Latino school, I had a first grade student, Isaac, with two moms. They were happy to help out, and that was a natural way to show Isaac and the whole class that having two moms was one of the many family constellations. We also had students living with grandparents, with single moms or dads, and in foster homes.

Teachers can get support for having such discussions from the films about different kinds of families, curriculum materials, and library books that are available.

Becki added,

> As a curriculum director, I made this part of new teacher training. We brought in speakers, often LGBT high school or college

students with similar ethnicities to our students, who shared how they were harassed on a daily basis, often beginning in elementary school. On one occasion, I brought a panel of high school students back to their own elementary school. One of the presenters said that she remembered her fifth grade teacher made a very simple general comment about the many types of couples and families in the world that included two men or two women and that was what made our world such a great place. That comment stuck with her, as she already began questioning her sexual orientation beginning in elementary school. The teacher, who was present in the session, never expected such a passing comment to make such an impact.

CHALLENGES AND DILEMMAS

Taking on the challenges and dilemmas of using diversity as a resource in a meaningful and powerful way involves

1. reframing the way we think about classroom diversity in the first place,

2. accepting the fact that it may seem like an overwhelming topic,

3. addressing race in the classroom, and

4. recognizing that whether we are teaching about race or not, we are actually always teaching about race and diversity.

Reframing the Way We Think About Classroom Diversity

The dilemma with reframing how we think about diversity is that it requires teachers to have the capacity to "know what they don't know." It means recognizing the ways that we might have approached student difference as a problem and shifting to think of it as a rich teaching resource. It means not being colorblind, but thinking about diversity as a positive element in the classroom—not one to be ignored. Further, the primary role of the teacher is not simply to prevent discrimination or name calling; it is to facilitate a process in which students get to know, respect, and depend on one another and to understand the various perspectives held by each other.

Consider When It Is Appropriate to Address Race in the Classroom

The first step is to become an observer of one's practice while being actively engaged. This is not an easy task, but it is needed to make a safe environment for all students. Student identity is continually shaped not only by the media and the family but also on the playground by fellow students or through subtle messages experienced vis-à-vis power dynamics in the classroom (Lewis, 2003). Teachers should not be reticent to address stereotyping issues "too early" because, just like other important concepts such as fairness and honesty, when students have experiences with racism or sexism they need help in understanding and learning what to do in a developmentally appropriate manner. Although it is hard to know exactly when and how to bring up issues of racism or sexism, groundwork needs to be laid to be ready to address it when a teachable moment occurs for students at any age.

Accept the Fact That It Seems Like an Overwhelming Topic

We have discussed many elements included in using diversity as a resource for teaching, and it may seem like an impossibly complex issue to tackle. It is true that our understandings and practices of social identities are in constant flux. But, as teachers develop in their own understanding, they will become more skilled at including these elements, such as working to create an equal, accepting, cooperative classroom where students get to know one another and learn to appreciate each other's various perspectives and histories. Teachers and students will become more confident in addressing overt racism or sexism when their efforts are seen as learning steps and not mistakes to be punished.

We Are Teaching About Race and Diversity, Whether We Intend to or Not

Finally, teachers are teaching about race, gender, and status whether they intend to or not. If we ignore difference or make it a problem, we are teaching that to the students. When students' life experiences are disregarded, it says to students that who you are and what you know do not matter here. When we group children for learning in color-coded ways, it says some students are smart and some are not. It gives the whole class the image that capacity is fixed and not enhanced by experience and practice. So, teachers, take courage and take charge of the messages you give your students, so they can learn, along with you, how to become more inclusive.

PUTTING DIVERSITY AS A RESOURCE FOR TEACHING INTO PRACTICE

1. Using diversity as a resource for teaching requires teachers to continually reflect on their own attitudes, behaviors, and identities.
   - Think about what makes you feel identity safe as a teacher in your building.

   - What experiences in school shaped your own identity as a student?

2. Students need to see themselves reflected in the curriculum, drawing both from their own personal lives, music, tradition, languages, and community role models and from the formal content of history and literature. Select two students and identify some natural ways to infuse their lives into the classroom.

Student	Cultural/Language Background	Activity

(Continued)

(Continued)

3. What are some ways to foster a process in which students of different racial, ethnic, and gender groups get to know one another and work as a team toward greater learning goals while still validating their differences?

Objective	Activity
Build a sense of team in your class	
Celebrate classroom diversity in the context of the whole group	

4. What are some age-appropriate ways you can help students to learn the value of multiple perspectives and to critically analyze content from a range of sources?

Objective of the Lesson	Activity
Respect differing opinions of their classmates	
Critically analyze history	
Critically analyze current events	
Learn about multiple global perspectives	

High Expectations and Academic Rigor 8

WHY HIGH EXPECTATIONS AND ACADEMIC RIGOR?

Combining high expectations with true academic rigor allows students to develop skills while building confidence and a stronger sense of competence. How many times have we been proven wrong by a child who surpassed our expectations? Are we communicating to our students that they are capable and that as their teachers we have high expectations for their success? Importantly, positive presuppositions—the assurance that we are confident in their capacity to learn—goes beyond isolated comments. Our assumptions are conveyed in every verbal and nonverbal message we give to our students, both individually and as a group.

Meera told the IDS study group that she worried that about Carlota, a shy and extremely perceptive girl who watched the other fifth grade students like a hawk and always compared herself to them. So Meera tried a new technique to communicate her expectations:

> I purposely walked by many times so I would actually catch a glimpse of something, and I'd point out, "Oh, that is really good, what you're doing." And Carlota looked at me like, "Oh! You mean I don't have to hide my work?"
>
> Sometimes in the beginning, she was fudging, and that was really hard. I had to tell her, "It's okay, and we don't have to know everything. If you're going to know everything in fifth grade when you come, what am I going to teach you? It would be so boring, because I won't have anything to teach you."

Karen (Grade 5) had a similar feeling about Armando. He was very thoughtful, but it took time for him to express himself, so often other students overshadowed him. She let him know that better ideas often emerge from slow, thoughtful consideration. She communicated her positive presupposition to Armando and then to the group:

> A strategy that worked with him was not allowing him to be invisible. I said, "Armando, I'm going to be checking in. I'd like to hear what you have to say about this. I value your opinions, I'm coming back to check on you, I'd like to hear what you have to say, you're never going to be invisible." Then I would say, "The group needs to hear from you, those are great ideas." I was making sure that he was heard with those great ideas, and I'd ask, "Can I share this with the class?" I would always ask him. I'd say to the class "Oh, Armando brought up this great idea!" At the end of the year, bless his heart, he raised his hand more.

Karen showed Armando that his ideas were valuable when she shared them with the entire class. This kind of validation is more powerful than generic praise, which can raise students' suspicions about the teacher's sincerity.

High expectations influence student learning only when coupled with academic rigor, achievement-oriented standards, and with the assumption that the students can meet the expectations. When teachers communicate that they believe the students are indeed capable, convey their rigorous expectations, and then scaffold instruction to help their students learn the challenging curriculum in a step-by-step manner, a sense of competence emerges. One way that teachers convince students that they are capable is by continuously making the link between effort and learning. This helps students see that success in learning is connected to their effort and dilutes the notion of students having fixed abilities (Dweck, 2006).

HIGH EXPECTATIONS AND ACADEMIC RIGOR: HOW TO DO IT

Hold High Expectations for All Students

A student can feel that the teacher likes her and still feel incompetent. This is because the teacher's liking may be accompanied by subtle messages of low expectations or no expectations at all. Becki, a former K–8 principal, remembers an experience that, in retrospect, was hard to believe. She was visiting a school in a high-achieving community and observed Jewel, a mainstreamed special education fourth grader, who was extremely far behind:

Though Jewel had a good relationship with her teacher, she was not learning anything. When observing in her classroom, I found Jewel happily crocheting, while the other students were doing math. Her teacher told me that she did not want Jewel to feel bad about being so far behind and so she made sure that Jewel would feel comfortable. Unfortunately, this was not addressing Jewel's academic growth and learning.

In an identity safe classroom, teachers build competence in the context of a caring community; however, it is crucial that the relationship extends *beyond* warmth and kindness. Student competence will increase as teachers provide learning experiences that involve them in engaging with new ideas and developing skills to analyze and interpret information. As students participate in incorporating and creating new knowledge, they will begin to see themselves as competent members of the classroom community.

Integrate Bloom's Taxonomy Into Curriculum on a Daily Basis

Using Bloom's taxonomy (Bloom, 1956) is one way for teachers to think about how to continuously include higher order questions in their practice. Bloom's taxonomy is a regular part of most preservice credential programs, but it is often neglected when teaching the standards that will be tested on standardized tests that do not focus on higher level thinking. Becki shared,

At first I found incorporating Bloom's higher level thinking skills a bit overwhelming. Then, after attending a workshop on effective instructional skills, I learned to make it a regular practice to include the level of thinking in every lesson objective for my first graders. In that way, I monitored how often I was asking students to analyze, synthesize, and evaluate. To ensure students' understanding, I asked them to turn to a partner and explain a concept in their own words. In that way, I was able to hear what students had learned and to monitor their understanding while providing them a useful method of assuring retention of new concepts.

I realized when teaching first grade that asking them to compare two of their favorite games and tell which they preferred and why was an example of evaluation. Once I realized that even young children can analyze, compare, and evaluate, I was able to offer many opportunities for students. For example, first graders had no trouble finding similarities and differences between the *Nutcracker* storybook and the actual ballet we went to see. In addition, we analyzed the stories we read and made Venn diagrams to help students analyze, compare, and evaluate. Once I demystified Bloom's taxonomy, I was able to make higher order thinking a regular part of my teaching.

Work Toward Mastery

Helping students focus on mastery, rather than on competition, helps them avoid concerns about winning or being right, so they can give full attention to learning the skills and concepts at hand. Students can help each other notice and celebrate improvement. Karen found a place on her wall to post the writing of each of her fifth graders. Each month she would place another piece of writing on top of the previous one. This was an easy way for the students to notice the continual improvement and the marked growth between the start and finish of the school year.

During math instruction, Meera's fifth graders moved beyond just getting the right answer by sharing their different approaches to solving a problem. Step-by-step, she taught a variety of strategies for solving problems and posted them on charts around the room. She highlighted the different ways students solved a problem, and together with the class, she analyzed the value in each of the strategies. They discussed which method was the fastest, which was least likely to have errors, and which led to new and ingenious solutions. She also encouraged students to invent new and different strategies.

Strategies such as those Karen and Meera used with their students allow teachers to demonstrate directly to students that persisting at work can result in improved outcomes. When teachers provide ongoing opportunities for students to reflect on and analyze their work and that of other students, the students see that learning is a developmental process. The spoken and implicit observation is that everyone improves with practice. The question is not who is smart and who is not, but how can each of us improve our skills and knowledge?

Scaffold Student Learning

The concept of scaffolding learning can be visualized by thinking of how a painter uses a scaffold to reach all the floors of a high building. As a painter can reach great heights with a scaffold, students can reach high levels of learning with scaffolding from teachers. It is defined as providing an appropriate degree of support to allow a child to become successful in a particular learning situation that might have otherwise been too difficult.

This concept draws from Vygotsky's (1978) "proximal zones of learning," the idea that beyond what students can do independently is a "zone" where a student can function with support. When teachers teach to that zone, students can continue to grow and achieve and continuously reach higher levels. Teachers begin by assessing what students already know, and starting from that point, they provide materials, instruction, and support to help the students understand the subsequent concept.

Teachers can prompt and scaffold students' thinking by asking a series of questions that probe deeper into their thinking. The key is to avoid rhetorical questions that can be answered without thinking as well as those that put students on the defensive. Directing questions to all students using Bloom's taxonomy will engage all members of the class in high-level thinking.

What we are talking about here is helping students engage in metacognitive thinking. *Metacognition* is thinking about thinking. This process is an important one in developing the next strategies in understanding something. Teachers can engage students in metacognitive thinking by explaining their own thinking as they initiate a lesson: "This is what I was intending to do when I did. . . ." They can also model and teach students to do strategic planning prior to starting a project and to follow up by analyzing the results. Teachers can also paraphrase students' thinking to ensure they clearly understand it, and they can get students to clarify their thinking when it is vague and unformed. Additionally, they can ask students to explain their thinking in words and later in writing. Also, analyzing errors is a practice that both acknowledges errors and serves as a learning experience that helps students thoughtfully identify more effective strategies.

Scaffolding works best when it is naturally built into the learning, as in providing leveled books that move students to new skill levels in small increments. Teachers scaffold student learning as they assess their students and find a book, project, or math problem to match each student's level. It works by providing a challenging curriculum at the appropriate level of instruction and giving students effective tools to achieve the standards. Students may be surprised by their new accomplishments. These accomplishments become the most powerful motivator.

Meera shared the following:

> At the end of fifth grade, I asked my class to reflect on what had contributed to their learning. It struck me because Andy wrote that I helped him make growth in reading "because you make me feel welcomed and also helped me by telling me to read more and by giving me harder literature books."

Scaffold English Learners

Scaffolding instruction allows English learners to be taught the same curriculum as students with a greater mastery of English. This scaffolding is done through very specific strategies for accessing content. Graphic organizers, visuals, and academic language are all scaffolds. For example, when teachers provide academic vocabulary for a particular lesson, students can gain the tools they need to learn new concepts. Not knowing words like *height* or *depth* will block understanding of a geometry lesson for students just learning English. Previewing the lesson by briefly summarizing what is to be learned provides a context for understanding the lesson.

A complete set of strategies for scaffolding for English learners goes beyond the scope of this book, but the purpose of this brief section is to show a few simple techniques and to highlight the need for such scaffolding for all students in identity safe classrooms.

Begin College and Career Readiness in Kindergarten

Students need to understand why doing well in school is linked to the purpose of education. In short, the goal of education is to promote students' learning and development so that they can become educated, participating citizens who are engaged in meaningful, economically sustaining work and family life. This is a big charge. Promoting lifelong learning and linking it to preparation for college and career helps give students a context for their learning. Starting in elementary school, students need to develop a college-going culture. Students whose parents have attended college may come to school with these expectations, automatically. However, the know-how for preparing for college and career needs to be cultivated and fostered for those whose parents did not attend college, particularly for English learners and those from low-income families. The link between their effort, high expectations, and the rigor required to be successful in school needs to be made explicit with ongoing information and support.

For example, Becki reported,

> A high school student who was born in Jamaica once told me that he realized in middle school that the other students in his seventh grade class came with a plan. They may not have known which college they planned to attend, but their parents had already instilled the goal of attending college and the plan for what middle school courses would be needed to get on that track to the best colleges.

When a student does not have or know how to seek out the support, she enters high school without adequate grades, preparation, and self-confidence to take and pass the needed courses. She may also not even know which courses are required for college. Many students, even those with acceptable grade point averages, find out too late they did not take the right courses.

Often a debate ensues among educators who claim that not all students need to attend college. However, the goal is to provide college readiness and prepare students to have options and choices when they finish high school. For students whose parents may not have finished high school, it may take years to instill a belief that college is in the future. Starting the conversation early in elementary school sets up expectations and preparation for these children.

Some schools forge a college-going culture by having classrooms "adopt" colleges and learn about college life starting in kindergarten. Teachers share about their college experiences and articulate the skills needed to be strong students and good thinkers, and they teach that persistence is needed to achieve at high levels. Parents should be provided checklists of what to expect and how to plan for college at different grade levels from elementary school through high school.

CHALLENGES AND DILEMMAS

When the IDS study group probed deeper into the challenges of creating high expectations in an identity safe classroom, they looked at three areas:

1. supporting students who are below grade level in ways that do not add to their negative self-perception as students,

2. countering students' low expectations and negative messages about their competence from others, and

3. undoing the damage of low expectations for students with a weakened sense of competence.

Supporting Students Who Are Below Grade Level

When working with students who need extra support, it is a balancing act to avoid contributing to their sense of not being smart. A child who constantly gets the wrong answers or is always being asked if she needs help wonders, "What is wrong with me?" Yet it does not do a service to a child to allow a misconception or error to continue just to protect her self-esteem. To assist her in correcting errors, yet avoiding frequent negative comments, teachers can give genuinely encouraging suggestions. They can acknowledge the student's effort, perseverance, and improvement. They can also highlight her competence regularly across a school day by applauding her other areas of strength, including character strengths like kindness, trustworthiness, and responsibility.

The group also needs to hear messages that place a value on persistence, practice, and learning from mistakes. This is done by exposing students to stories about great athletes and musicians who practice for hours on end to achieve their expertise. Teachers can share their personal stories and those of other role models who do not give up after failing, like that of world-famous Michael Jordan, who did not initially make his high school basketball team and went on to be a basketball star; and Abraham Lincoln, who ran for public office and lost many times on his path to the presidency. Ultimately, it is a special skill to communicate your belief in your students and help all of them find their own strengths and gain a personal sense of competence.

Undoing the Damage of Low Expectations

The IDS study group talked about the students whose experience at school may have led to their having low expectations for themselves. For these students, a teacher must redouble efforts to build trust and rebuild confidence in their competence. Karen (Grade 5) brought up the issue of students who internalized negative messages about their intelligence. She felt the solution was to counter the powerful messages about intelligence that may be prevalent at home and on the schoolyard, by bringing up the issue in advance. She set a class norm to not say the "s-word" (*stupid*) and explicitly taught students not to undermine each other's sense of competence:

> The s-word, or *stupid*, is not allowed in the room. That is mentioned on day one. I don't think it's a good descriptor of anything, except for what we call author's privilege. So, Gilly Hopkins (Patterson, 1978), a character in my students' literature book, says *stupid*, and then we talk about it. Why did the author choose that word? And so it kind of ends up being a talking point for how use of the word *stupid* gets carried out into other words, like *idiot*, and it is highly judgmental. So, every time someone says *stupid*, they'll gasp and say, "That wasn't right."

Karen's intent, when giving messages to students about their own abilities, also included a metacognitive focus: helping students learn to analyze their own feelings in the context of deeply held societal views about intelligence. She helped them shift to new ways of understanding intelligence by overtly dispelling the myths together with teaching them to recognize their own intellectual and academic growth. For identity safe teachers, one way to address this challenge is to discuss *competence* with their students and explain the danger in undermining it.

Countering Low Expectations and Negative Messages About Competence

Negative messages about competence come from many sources. Sometimes peers make remarks like, "That was a dumb thing to say." Siblings compete in families, such as when a younger sister has better grades than her older brother and says, "I am smarter than you." The media continually give messages about intelligence with films like *Dumb and Dumber* and shows that make fun of the "dumbest criminal" or compare viewers to others, such as *Are You Smarter Than a Fifth Grader?*

Becki shared,

> I know that parents want the best for their children, but sometimes they do not realize that casual comments can undermine a student's sense of himself. I remember a parent saying to her son, "*No seas burro*" (don't be a dumb donkey), and another parent who said, "My sons are gifted, but my daughter is just average."

Many parents who have not been exposed to Carol Dweck's concept of the "growth mindset," the notion that intelligence is malleable and changes with learning, can unintentionally do serious damage to their children (Dweck, 2006). Becki's IDS study group members realized the need to bring parents along as they worked on identity safety and student competence. Karen (Grade 5) explained how she introduced the incremental view of intelligence at parent conferences:

> You can help these parents understand and say, "Listen, these are the great attributes your child has. There are different kinds of intelligences—yes, there are some weaknesses here, yes, we need to work on that, but look at what we have here. Let's use these stronger ones to build up confidence and strengthen the weaker ones up. It's OK to have different kinds of intelligences."

Ann shared that beyond teaching positive ways to help her second graders think about intelligence, she had an experience in which a parent's dangerous misunderstanding about her child's learning needs deeply impacted the daughter:

> Claribel was identified for special education. Her mom spoke Spanish and didn't understand the test results very well. The next day her daughter came to school in tears. Her mother had gone home and told her something was wrong with her brain.

Ann attempted to undo the damage by clarifying to the child and parent that having a learning disability did not mean she was not smart. Ann explained that Claribel learned differently and showed her mother ways to support Claribel by meeting her learning needs.

Teachers need to partner with parents to teach them how to build, rather than undermine, their children's expectations for themselves. It means not belittling their children or comparing their children to others. Some parents have limited education and do not feel competent themselves. Thus, it is important for teachers to discuss with parents their belief in the child's potential and to offer evidence of that potential. Then teachers can show parents how to encourage their children. At the same time, teachers need to be careful about how they speak to the parents, by modeling the same respect toward parents that they are encouraging parents to have with their children. Others on the campus also need to learn these ideas. Otherwise, a teacher's efforts might be undermined or diluted by negative and judgmental messages about intelligence from others on campus.

PUTTING HIGH EXPECTATIONS AND ACADEMIC RIGOR INTO PRACTICE

1. In identity safe classrooms, teachers work to build trust while nurturing and motivating students. What are some initial contacts you can make to build trust with each of your students? For example, are there ways to greet the students as they arrive in the classroom that show you are glad they are there and show your high expectations that they will have a productive day as learners?

2. What are some ways that teachers inadvertently create a culture of competition in the classroom? How can you work to create a noncompetitive environment?

3. One of the greatest challenges teachers face is meeting the academic needs of students at different skill levels *and* communicating high expectations. What are some learning tasks you might include in teaching reading, writing, and speaking that involve all of the students regardless of initial skill level? For example, can students work together in "mixed-skill" groups to rewrite a new end to a story that would be more fair, or more realistic, or happier?

This tool is also available for download at **www.corwin.com/identitysafe.**

Challenging Curriculum

9

WHY CHALLENGING CURRICULUM?

Due to the increasing pressure on schools to raise their test scores, the focus of teaching has shifted. The notion of providing a challenging curriculum is often lost, as teachers feel forced to restrict the curriculum to enable students to score well on high-stakes multiple-choice tests. Teachers spend an inordinate amount of instructional time on test preparation, particularly in schools with high numbers of students of color. One study reported that teachers spent up to 60% of class time on "test-prep" (Advancement Project, 2010, p. 6). This leads to less time on deep learning that could provide students with the knowledge and skills needed for a successful transition to college and careers.

Another result of this focus on test prep is that dropout rates are actually increasing. According to the Advancement Project,

> In 2006, the nation's graduation rate was the lowest it has been since before NCLB was passed. Of particular concern is that the graduation rates for Black and Latino students—51% and 55%, respectively, dropped significantly from 2005 to 2006. Additionally, in 2008, the number of persons taking the GED test was at its highest level since before NCLB. These are all strong indicators of a rampant student push-out problem. (Advancement Project, 2010, p. 6)

Another result of the dominant focus on raising test scores is the hijacking of a challenging curriculum to an instructional focus on the mastery of a laundry list of standards. There are not enough hours in the school day to adequately teach all content standards, and so time constraints lead to teaching only what will be tested (Darling-Hammond, 2010).

This results in narrowing the focus to math and literacy often to the exclusion of the arts, science, and physical education. A study of science education in California's elementary schools revealed that 80% of students were receiving less than 60 minutes of science instruction per week, and 16% were receiving no science instruction at all. These were mostly the schools in Program Improvement (California's term for schools whose students have scored inadequately on standardized tests); their staffs reported that they were so busy raising math and reading scores that they had no time to teach science (Dorph et al., 2007).

In contrast, Linda Darling-Hammond, professor at Stanford University, describes what top-performing countries have done to provide a challenging curriculum for all students. For example, Singapore has radically transformed its entire educational system since 1979 to create what it calls a "thinking schools, learning nation." This reformed curriculum incorporates the arts, music, and a focus on creativity and innovation. The number of content standards was reduced to allow for in-depth learning, and tests were upgraded to incorporate higher order thinking. Similarly, other top-performing countries have fewer content standards, according to the Trends in International Math and Science Study (Olson, Martin, & Mullis, 2008). These countries teach fewer standards per year, which results in deeper learning with less redundancy and repetition.

Closer to home, Professor Darling-Hammond finds that schools and districts that are successful in teaching all students use assessments with a greater focus on critical thinking and problem solving. Their curricula draw upon students' interests and knowledge, authentic reading materials are used, and a range of supports is provided for scaffolding that include explicit instruction combined with carefully crafted small group inquiry and coached independent projects (Darling-Hammond, 2010).

We propose the following four-part approach to implementing challenging curriculum in diverse classrooms. First, focus on creating an air of intellectual excitement. Second, offer an appropriate level of challenge for each student, while encouraging students to ask for help. Third, make classrooms a safe place for thinking, and finally, differentiate instruction to include high levels of thinking for all students.

CHALLENGING CURRICULUM: HOW TO DO IT

Create an Air of Intellectual Excitement

What makes for an air of intellectual excitement? Not unlike a fire, it needs kindling to get started. The kindling needs to be in the form of relevant connections that link to a child's life. From there, a fire needs air to breathe. That could be the open-ended activities that allow for the mind to be creative. A fire needs a source of fuel—meaningful tasks that require high levels of thinking and doing. Finally, once the fire has caught on, the teacher's role is to stoke it through questioning, asking for hypotheses, inference, and deduction.

There are many ways to reach children with a range of learning styles. The key is to put all these pieces together. Becki recalls,

> Although I was never a science buff, my high school physics teacher created that "air of intellectual excitement" in his classroom by giving us interesting problems to solve with physics. I still remember the bag of lenses he placed on the table followed by the challenge of figuring out why the image was flipped upside down in a convex lens. These are the experiences in school that stay with you. When I became a teacher, I incorporated the same kinds of questions into my curriculum.

Inquiry learning is exciting and highly motivating and is more likely to be retained as students make personal connections to new discoveries.

In Julia's fifth grade class, an exciting debate ensued as students took a textbook question and dug into it deeply. The question was whether covered wagons were more reliable than cars for coming west. Julia began with the assumption that students would immediately recognize that cars were more reliable. Perhaps because her students had had bad experiences with cars breaking down and with not having enough money for high-priced gasoline, they didn't buy a quick answer. Instead, they asked poignant questions and posed interesting arguments for why the reverse might be true. The actual answer was less important than the excitement in the room as students grappled with the question. Julia had created a space in her classroom that sparked this kind of discussion. She encouraged divergent thinking, listened to the students, and responded in ways that considered their point of view valuable rather than shutting down the dissention.

Rarely, if ever, does a textbook or computer program alone provide all the ingredients needed for successful teaching. Teachers need to build connections to prior knowledge, entice students with interesting activities, and add additional materials to the mix, beyond what is available in the textbook. Today, with amazing Internet resources, students have access to information from across the globe and primary sources from throughout history. Teachers also have access to lesson plans, videos, and ideas on any topic imaginable and can capture the excitement with a varied recipe of information and engagement. One of many examples is PBS LearningMedia (http://www.pbslearningmedia.org/), a free collection of thousands of public education films with lesson guides on a wide range of topics. Another valuable resource is Edutopia (http://www.edutopia.org), also a collection of best practices and teaching tools with ideas for project-based learning and social-emotional learning.

Provide an Appropriate Level of Challenge and Encourage Students to Ask for Help

The members of the IDS study group asked themselves whether the lesson was at the appropriate level of challenge—neither too easy nor too hard. This requires knowing the students well and the range of performance levels in the classroom. Karen (Grade 5) described this challenge in terms of Armando:

> My "Armandos" are my most puzzling students, because they're quiet and they'll never tell me exactly what they need and why. It's me having to kind of cajole to find out. With self-directed kids, if you have a project proposal, well great, let's take a look, whereas he would never come with a proposal.

When the IDS study group members observed Jennifer, a sixth grade teacher who had participated in the research district's study group on identity safety, they saw how she shifted the culture of her classroom to help her students who originally were afraid to admit mistakes in their math. Jennifer told her students that examining mistakes was one of the best ways to truly learn a new concept. She invented a game of asking who wanted to share an error. A student put his work up on the board while the rest of the class scrambled to figure out how the mistake in thinking had occurred. Because this was a regular part of the class routine, many hands shot up when Jennifer asked for volunteers. This game helped Jennifer's students understand that being intelligent does not mean you know everything.

Karen modeled to her class that mistakes are part of everyone's learning process by humorously pointing to her own blunders.

In a different approach, Meera created a safe, private space at a back table for her fifth grade students to get help. Students of all academic levels soon sought the extra support:

> What I do is let them know that whoever needs extra help can find me at the back table, or you can just sit with me and work

when you don't want to do it independently; it's okay. I sit over there, by myself with a math book. Isn't it funny who shows up, sometimes it's your advanced kids who just want to hang out. In the beginning, Yesenia used to pretend that she knew everything. She never came for help at the back table. Then Yesenia started realizing you didn't have to be stupid in math to be there. So, she started coming too.

Students begin to take risks and enjoy the challenge of learning when they realize that everyone makes errors and that by asking for help, they can learn from their mistakes. In the IDS study group, we reminded ourselves that when students see us as models, when they do not feel judged and are willing to take risks, they develop competence. When they feel belonging and engagement and are willing to participate, they feel more confident and they experience more success in a continuous reciprocal relationship.

Make Classrooms Safe Places for Thinking

Grouping students for learning is a nuanced process that makes a big difference in how safe they feel to participate, and in how they respond to one another and to the task at hand. Teachers should keep in mind the purpose of the task and the goal for having students work together. For example, can the students actually help one another? Does this grouping provide a chance for students to get to know students they may be less familiar with in the classroom? Is there anything about the group's composition that might make a student feel more or less well regarded? Students learn to feel safe to think broadly when they have numerous chances to say and hear a variety of ideas from their classmates on a regular basis.

Becki described,

Sometimes I created a critical mass of one language group, and at other times, I would have partners with very different backgrounds. I deliberately mixed it up so many different ways that they could not see a pattern or feel I was tracking them in any way. Groupings were based on similar backgrounds, learning styles, academic levels, interests, and at rare times, friendships. Often, I purposely made random groups of mixed performance levels. I called these groupings "mixing the pot," because the different groupings drew on the richness of the diversity in the classroom.

By mixing the groups, teachers can check any preconceived notions they might have about their students and can help reduce the possibility of unintentionally creating a sense of stereotype threat in some of their students.

Differentiate Instruction to Offer Higher Level Thinking for All Students

Differentiation is a way to teach to a range of academic levels in one classroom, enabling each student to achieve at high levels. The goal is to ensure that all students are challenged, regardless of their present academic level. Motivating all students to reach and surpass grade-level standards means finding out where each one is and building from that point. As one of the most challenging aspects of teaching, differentiation demands a deep knowledge of each child's skills and learning style combined with flexible management strategies.

The challenge of differentiation is to be flexible in using all available tools and management strategies to guarantee that each student steadily progresses during all lessons. Tools include (1) assessment and monitoring of each student's knowledge in all subject areas, (2) instructional strategies that target different learning styles, and (3) groupings that vary, including creating partnerships with other teachers for departmentalized lessons (Tomlinson & McTigue, 2006).

Tomlinson and McTigue (2006) suggest differentiating instruction not just based on academic level but also on interest area and learning style. This model ensures that students work on their weaknesses and also are motivated by drawing from their strengths and personal interests. When teachers consider variation in student learning styles, they can encourage students to use new ways to solve problems. Remember not to designate one style or another to individual students. Learning styles, like other attributes, are not fixed, and we want to help young minds develop a flexible approach to problem solving and creative thinking.

Lessons also can be differentiated by content, process, and product (Tomlinson & McTigue, 2006). *Content* can be differentiated by providing information at different reading levels, using jigsaw models, or letting children choose a topic of interest. *Process* can be differentiated by providing hands-on lessons, adaptive computer programs, different groupings, and different levels of assistance by teachers, paraprofessionals, or peers. *Products* can be differentiated to include written, graphic, and multimedia individual and group presentations that may or may not be integrated with the arts.

These varied purposes of differentiation lend themselves to differing student groupings as described above. To make sure these strategies are effective, the class needs training in how to work independently, in partners, and in teams to allow the teacher the flexibility to work with individuals and small groups. Students need specific expectations for every aspect of this process. They need to learn acceptable noise levels, how to get needed materials, how to manage their time, and how to get help when the teacher is working with a group. Without strong management strategies, differentiation would lead to a waste of time for students who are not working with the teacher.

Thus, the teacher herself needs to learn how to focus on a small group with an ear and eye to what the rest of the students are doing. This can be accomplished by affording lots of practice with the class working independently without the teacher during the small groups. Then the class can self-evaluate both before and after the teacher works with groups. Students are proud of themselves when they learn to work autonomously and effectively.

Whole-group instruction can be differentiated as well. Questioning strategies can allow for deepening knowledge and higher level thinking, making the content accessible for all students. For example, ask students to think in a metacognitive manner (e.g., "How did you figure out the answer?"). Mix the questions to vary rote learning, with inferential questions and questions that ask students for their opinions or feelings on a topic. Asking the students to formulate their own questions helps them engage more deeply with the content. Pair-share activities and white boards or quick-writes actively engage each child in the lesson. Teachers can circulate to monitor students for understanding. Have them turn to a neighbor and define or explain an idea in their own words to help with retention. Students need to be actively engaged at least once every 10 minutes or so when teachers are providing whole-group instruction.

We suggest that teachers make a deeper inquiry into differentiating instruction, because the ability to reach each student at her level in a culture of equal status is one of the foundational principles of identity safety.

CHALLENGES AND DILEMMAS

In this section, we will discuss the following challenges and dilemmas teachers face as they implement a challenging curriculum:

1. getting started with meaningful differentiation,

2. ensuring students at all performance levels use higher level thinking, and

3. breaking the cycle of repeated failure.

Getting Started With Meaningful Differentiation

The transition to differentiated instruction does not occur overnight and needs to be thought out carefully. Becki shared a dilemma they faced in her school:

> The need to differentiate is widely recognized, but textbooks still cater to a direct instruction model where whole classes are taught the same lesson by a teacher standing in front of the classroom. In our professional development, we learned that after a 45-minute whole-group direct instruction lesson, we need to catch some students up with content they may have missed. At that time, we were to work with English learners or students who were behind by preteaching upcoming content or reteaching content that might not have been retained. The other students are given required independent work or additional enrichment activities.
>
> However, in my experience this model was problematic and very difficult to implement. My main concern was that we were supposed to spend most class time teaching lessons to the whole group that were either too hard for part of the class or too easy for others and therefore a waste of time for up to two thirds of the students. Conversely, there was too little time later in the day to allow me to catch anyone up, so the low-performing students got even further behind.

If teachers work together, they can take initial steps toward meaningful differentiation. Becki shared this example:

> At my school, we began with small group reading in the computer lab. The teacher pulled small groups for leveled reading while the other students used adaptive computer programs supported by a paraprofessional aide. Even this was a challenge, but that was a good place to start.

The important thing is that both the small group working with the teacher and the rest of the class are engaged in meaningful learning activities. The Common Core State Standards do not specify instructional strategies, but the "sit and get" model of whole-class instruction will never allow all students to arrive at the level of depth and rigor the standards are designed to develop.

Higher Level Thinking for Students at All Performance Levels

Higher level thinking and challenging curriculum is for students at *all* performance levels. Some teachers think that only the "gifted" students can think at higher levels. It is unfortunate when teachers approach learning as a ladder, where knowing basic skills is the prerequisite before any higher levels of synthesis, analysis, and evaluation are offered. In schools where the students are primarily English learners and low-income students, higher levels are forfeited for a focus on basic skills. Basic knowledge and higher level thinking are not mutually exclusive and can be woven into a dynamic curriculum.

Because learning is both a cognitive and social-psychological process, it is important, indeed, necessary, for teachers to help students make connections between what they know and what they are learning. If what is being taught has no meaning to students, or is totally isolated from their own experience, their learning will be reduced to memorizing facts, at best. They will not be motivated or excited about the content and will not become involved in the process of constructing new understandings.

Though it is true that certain levels of knowledge and skills are needed for students to analyze or synthesize new information, the combination of learning the basics while putting it into meaningful practice will motivate them to achieve. Those who do not yet possess all the skills should not be left out of the process of learning complex concepts. Students with limited English or reading skills can respond verbally or work in groups to solve certain problems or come up with new understandings of material. When these students are taught only basic skills, they are forced to remain in a world of rote learning and repetitive work sheets, and they never truly apply their knowledge in new and unguided situations. It is when they are asked to apply their knowledge, analyze a situation, or evaluate from a choice of options—whether it is in math, literature, or science—that they truly begin to think for themselves and their intellectual curiosity is piqued.

Breaking the Cycle of Failure

Motivating a student who has experienced repeated failure is one of the most rewarding, yet difficult, aspects of teaching. Depending on how a teacher responds, even a single negative experience or failure can raise or lower a student's belief in herself and her capacities. In Karen's class, Elena, a fifth grade student with limited English skills, was caught cheating on a spelling test. Karen understood that Elena cheated because she did not want to fail or look bad. Karen took the situation seriously, yet rather than shame or belittle Elena, she spoke to Elena in private and was empathetic, saying, "I understand you want others to believe you are smart, but cheating is not the way to get there." Karen helped Elena see that, through effort, she could be successful. She also asked Elena to determine an appropriate consequence. Elena decided to write an essay using the spelling words from the test she cheated on, so she would be sure to learn them.

The incident constituted a turning point for Elena, who subsequently improved academically and became a positive leader in the classroom. Karen's approach to that disciplinary situation let Elena know that beyond any doubt, Karen cared about her *and* believed that Elena was a capable student who did not need to cheat on spelling tests, which she never did again. Karen commented that when students realize that someone believes in them, even when they are not successful, a transformation is possible.

PUTTING CHALLENGING CURRICULUM INTO PRACTICE

1. Think of two students: one who is ahead and one who is behind the others. How will you help build each student's sense of academic and social competence while equalizing student status?

2. What are two different ways that you can group your students for math? How will they help one another? How might they learn more by working together?

Part III Summary

In these three chapters on cultivating diversity as a resource for teaching and learning, we propose a rigorous, inclusive, and interwoven approach to practicing diversity in the classroom. This approach is based on two fundamental notions: One, teaching and learning is a social process based on relationships, and two, given the social nature of learning, who the students are and who the teacher is are important resources for the classroom. These two notions contain implications for practice.

The first is that it is essential for teachers to know their students and provide opportunities to help students know and trust their classmates. Students can help one another learn and inspire each other in a trusting, intellectually compelling, noncompetitive class where multiple perspectives are valued.

Second, through real knowledge of students and what they know and can do, teachers can set high expectations for each of the students and provide learning experiences that depend on rigorous academic work for every student. Though students may be at different levels of skills, when teachers focus on learning toward mastery rather than academic competition, every student can participate in genuine academic work. Teachers can help motivate and teach students by analyzing mistakes, scaffolding students' efforts by asking deeper questions, and giving help when needed.

The reason we include the idea that teachers should provide a challenging curriculum in diverse classes is that when students are provided with less, they will develop less academically. And, through many current practices of tracking and remediation, students of color are too often given less. Providing a challenging curriculum is the most difficult aspect of cultivating diversity in the classroom, because it requires teachers to differentiate instruction, to scaffold student learning with an understanding of how knowledge is culturally constructed, to provide various modes of teaching with an eye to equity pedagogy, and to shift the practice of finding the best students to helping all students do their best. When students feel equal status in the classroom and have the expectation that they can learn and that what they know and can do matters, an air of intellectual excitement will grow, further inspiring learning.

Finally, we talk directly about a noncolorblind approach to diversity, one that is rich in materials, experiences, and learning tasks that reflect the different lives of the students. When students see themselves reflected in the daily life of the class, they can trust that they belong there and have something to offer. Students who feel they really belong will be more willing to take risks and make mistakes, thereby increasing their social and academic competence.

Part III References

Advancement Project. (2010). *Test, punish, and push out* (Rev. ed.). Washington, DC, and Los Angeles, CA: Author.

Allport, G. (1954). *The nature of prejudice.* Cambridge, MA: Addison-Wesley.

Ambady, N., Shih, M., Kim, A., & Pitinsky, T. (2001). Stereotype susceptibility in children: Effects of identity activation on quantitative performance. *Psychological Science, 12*(5), 385–390.

Aronson, J., & Steele, C. M. (2005). Stereotypes and the fragility of academic competence, motivation, and self-concept. In A. J. Elliot & C. Dweck (Eds.), *Handbook of competence and motivation* (pp. 436–456). New York, NY: Guilford Press.

Banks, C., & Banks, J. (2003). *Handbook of research on multicultural education.* San Francisco, CA: Jossey-Bass.

Bloom, B. S. (1956). *Taxonomy of educational objectives: The classification of educational goals. Handbook I. Cognitive Domain.* New York, NY: David McKay.

Darling-Hammond, L. (2010). *The flat world and education: How America's commitment to equity will determine our future.* New York, NY: Teachers College Press.

Dorph, R., Goldstein, D., Lee, S., Lepori, K., Schneider, S., & Venkatesan, S. (2007). *The status of science education in the Bay Area: Research study e-report.* Berkeley: University of California.

Dovidio, J. F., & Gaertner, S. L. (2000). *Reducing intergroup bias: The common in-group identity model.* Philadelphia, PA: Psychology Press.

Drakeford, W. (2006). *Racial disproportionality in school disciplinary practices* (Practitioner brief). Tempe, AZ: National Center for Culturally Responsive Educational Systems. Retrieved from http://www.nccrest.org/Briefs/School_Discipline_Brief.pdf

Dweck, C. S. (2006). *Mindset: The new psychology of success.* New York, NY: Random House.

Elliot, A. J., & Dweck, C. S. (Eds.). (2005). Competence and motivation: Competence as the core of achievement motivation. In A. J. Elliot & C. S. Dweck (Eds.), *Handbook of competence and motivation* (pp. 436–456). New York, NY: Guilford Press.

Lee, E., Menkart, D., & Okazawa-Rey, M. (1997). *Beyond heroes and holiday: A practical guide for K–12 anti-racist, multicultural education and staff development.* Washington, DC: Network of Educators on the Americas.

Lewis, A. E. (2003). *Race in the schoolyard: Negotiating the color line in classrooms and communities.* New Brunswick, NJ: Rutgers University Press.

Markus, H. R., Steele, C. M., & Steele, D. M. (2000). Colorblindness as a barrier to inclusion: Assimilation and nonimmigrant minorities. *Daedalus, 129*(4), 233–259.

Nieto, S. (1998). *Affirmation, solidarity and critique: Moving beyond tolerance in education.* Washington DC: Network of Educators on the Americas.

Olson, J. F., Martin, M. O., & Mullis, I. V. S. (Eds.). (2008). *Technical report.* Trends in International Math and Science Study. Chestnut Hill, MA: TIMSS & PIRLS International Study Center, Boston College.

Patterson, K. (1978). *The Great Gilly Hopkins.* New York, NY: HarperCollins.

Pettigrew, T. F., & Tropp, L. R. (2005). Allport's intergroup contact hypothesis. In J. F. Dovidio, P. Click, & L. A. Rudman (Eds.), *On the nature of prejudice, fifty years after Allport* (pp. 262–277). New York, NY: Springer-Verlag.

Reno, J. (2006). Videogame: Over the (border) line. *Newsweek periscope.* Retrieved from http://www.msnbc.msn.com/id/12554978/site/newsweek/

Steele, D. M. (2012). *Identity-safe school environments, creating.* In J. A. Banks (Ed.), *Encyclopedia of diversity in education* (Vol. 1), 1125–1128. Thousand Oaks, CA: Sage

Tatum, B. D. (1997). *Why are all the black kids sitting together in the cafeteria?* New York, NY: Basic Books.

Tomlinson, C., & McTigue, J. (2006). *Integrating differentiated instruction and understanding by design.* Alexandria, VA: ASCD.

Vygotsky, L. S. (1978). *Mind in society: The development of higher psychological processes.* Cambridge, MA. Harvard University Press.

Part IV
Classroom Relationships

WHAT DO WE MEAN BY CLASSROOM RELATIONSHIPS?

Positive relationships, both between the teacher and students and among students, are the foundation of an identity safe classroom. Positive relationships lead to a sense of social belonging and connection to others. The need to belong and feel connected to others is a powerful motivating force and a basic human need. Whether we are being nourished, motivated, and challenged; or conversely angered, blamed or hurt over and over again; our relationships are constantly shaping our perceptions, thoughts, and feelings (Goleman, 2006). Children who may be vulnerable because of their social identities or some difficult life circumstance such as illness or homelessness require special attention to meet their needs for belonging in school.

Social support is linked to mental and physical health and many positive outcomes. A series of studies conducted by Greg Walton and Geoff Cohen (2007) and Claude Steele (2010) demonstrate the strong link between having a sense of belonging and student academic success. Because teaching and learning is a social process based on trusting relationships, all students share this need for belonging. Thus, teachers of students who have been marginalized in some way or whose ability at school has been negatively stereotyped have to examine their classrooms each day to determine that their relationships, practices, and curriculum are not inadvertently promoting a sense of stereotype threat but are confirming a sense of belonging. That means that teachers must regularly look at their relationship with each student, look at the students' relationships with one another, and confirm that the learning opportunities are meaningful and challenging for all students (Steele, C. M., 2010; Walton & Cohen, 2007).

There is another important outcome for students in socially supportive classrooms. The social dynamics in such a class help students learn to be caring, responsive, and responsible people. Instead of a vibe of competition—winner-takes-all—students can begin to see that learning is a process that often includes mistakes and giving and getting help. This approach can help students feel intellectually and socially safe and uncouple the link between the students' social identity and school success.

Meera (Grade 5) stated emphatically that there could be no formulaic checklist for creating the sense of belonging in an identity safe classroom. Rather, she suggests that teachers need to do the following:

> Get to know each student personally and keep communication open and honest, daily! The little things do matter. Show them you genuinely care and have high expectations for all children in your class.

Positive relationships are built on trust. Building trust comes from hundreds of affirming microinteractions. It is important to uncover positive qualities in each child and reveal hidden strengths. Meera explained, "Little conversations show children that you actually know their strengths, that you actually were listening and paying attention, and that you care enough to actually notice."

In an identity safe classroom, teachers work to find each student's strengths, even those of a student who annoys everyone or constantly interrupts the class. With this level of empathy and support, teachers can draw out a child's positive qualities and appreciate something about each of them that previously had been taken for granted. Not only the child but also the other students will be able to see that child differently after the hidden strengths are acknowledged. Positive classroom relationships are based on observable, intentional behaviors that occur when teachers show warmth, are accessible and supportive of student learning, and promote positive student relationships (Steele, D. M., 2012). In the following two chapters, we will address the factors that we found were linked to positive classroom relationships in the Stanford Integrated Schools Project (SISP) study. We will explain why each of these factors is important and will give examples of how to put them into practice. We will also highlight some challenges, contradictions, and messy aspects that form a natural part of human interactions.

Teacher Warmth **10** and Availability to Support Learning

WHY TEACHER WARMTH AND AVAILABILITY TO SUPPORT LEARNING?

A teacher's relationship with students incorporates two identity safety factors: Teacher Warmth and Availability to Support Learning. We put these two factors into one chapter because we want to show the strong relationship between the cognitive and social aspects of learning. Understanding this relationship will help teachers focus on both aspects, cognitive and social, as they work to help students learn. One can think of Teacher Warmth as a focus on the socioemotional life of the classroom, and Availability to Support Learning as a focus on academic efforts of the classroom. Each of these two factors has a unique quality and special significance for identity safety. A teacher can be warm and yet not provide adequate academic support for students. Conversely, a teacher could offer support to students while being distant and even cold.

Teachers demonstrate warmth to students when they show sincere appreciation for and pleasure in student efforts and accomplishments, relate personally to students, pay attention to their comments, and use humor freely. Importantly, Teacher Warmth is directed toward all students in the classroom, even those who may be struggling academically or socially. In an identity safe classroom, Teacher Warmth is characterized by the friendly tone and kind words the teacher uses with the students as individuals and the class as a whole. It includes expressions of pleasure, humor, and delight as well as appreciation for the students. The teacher works to make students feel comfortable. These behaviors are in contrast to highly critical, negative, and impersonal relationships with students.

The teacher avoids sarcasm and expressions of irritation or annoyance. This does not mean that the feeling tone is always pleasant. If a teacher needs to be firm, he focuses on specific desired behaviors and steers away from critical or blaming comments. He seeks to make learning challenging and engaging and the classroom an easy and comfortable place to be. In these classrooms, students can feel secure in their attempts to learn and participate as appreciated members of the classroom.

Teachers demonstrate that they are available to students and support them in their efforts to learn when they, the teachers, are genuinely engaged in classroom activities and demonstrate responsiveness to student needs and preferences. Encouraging students to seek help shows students that teachers understand that learning is a process that requires effort, practice, revision, and support from others. Praise and encouragement of their efforts and intentions allows them to feel that their teacher is there to help them succeed. When a student can count on his teacher to intervene in any academic or social situation when needed, he will feel that, as one of Karen's students told her, "I know you have my back!" Even the language he used was symbolic in its evidence that he knows his teacher "gets" how he speaks.

TEACHER WARMTH AND AVAILABILITY TO SUPPORT LEARNING: HOW TO DO IT

Connect With Each Student Daily

In identity safe classrooms, teachers make intentional efforts to personally connect with the students and provide constant support for their learning.

Ricardo, a third grade teacher, personally shook each child's hand and wished him or her well after class each day. He began this ritual after a tragedy where two of his students were struck by a car and killed in front of the school. He wanted to make sure that every single day he welcomed each student. He realized that this daily connection brought him closer to his class as a whole. This closeness with each of the students led to a class that was easier to manage. Our interpretation is that when students really feel they belong and are regarded well by the teacher, it is easier for them to manage their own behavior—to *act* like they belong.

Karen explained how she used a variety of ways to be personally connected to her fifth grade students:

> I find the most that I learn about students is at lunchtime. I have lunch dates with a coupon drawing to have lunch with me. At lunch

dates or if you interact on the yard, so much comes out. I say, "Hey, what are you guys playing? That looks fun."

Provide Support by Staying Close

Indirect management strategies also work well with specific students. Linda helped one of her sixth grade students, who had been transferred many times, manage his own behavior:

> I began the intervention with seating the student up front, nearest my primary teaching location. Proximity to me allowed for the constant supervision needed to control his disruptive classroom behaviors like yelling out and engaging neighboring students in off-task activity. When this was controlled in the first couple of days, my proximity enabled the student to begin to tackle work-avoidance habits such as fiddling with items lying on the desk, slouching in the chair, and putting his sweatshirt hood up. It quickly became clear that constant supervision might be replaced by systematic reminders.

At that point Linda created a *Student Success Chart* (Takimoto, 2006), so her transfer student could recognize his behavior and learn to monitor it. Linda reported,

> He slowly allowed me to attend consistently to behavior that prevented learning, eventually dropping any negative feedback, and took on responsibility for identifying personal behavior with the *Student Success Chart*. By mid-November, he was socializing positively and successfully with peers in the classroom and at recess and had formed the beginnings of a few friendships. He scored a proficient 83% on his end of November benchmark assessment!

Linda found that his engagement and completion of work steadily increased, and that "greater positive feedback socially from peers and academically from class performance and assessments were motivating the continued improvement for this student." Although Linda closely directed his learning, and the process of increasing autonomy was slow, his first independent step, completing the student success chart, helped him begin to take responsibility for his learning.

Linda used a variety of reminders with her students, including a prearranged private reminder known only to the individual student and herself. These types of reminders build mutual trust because the student feels his teacher has confidence that he will use the signal and comply.

A private reminder neither humiliates the student nor disrupts instruction. In time, the reminders can taper off as the student is able to control his own behavior.

Use Words Thoughtfully: They Are Powerful

Becki's daughter, who was always an excellent student, got a D on a progress report shortly after being in a serious car accident. The school counselor, who knew nothing about her or her life, suggested that she might be better off not going to a four-year college. Luckily, Becki was able to support her daughter and assure her that this counselor's erroneous assessment did not overshadow her years of academic success.

Such an incident, unfortunately, is not unusual for many students of color. These students are often guided toward less education and lower aspirations. One man, now serving as a dean at a leading university, was told to avoid college and try to become a plumber when he met with his high school counselor. Too many students are crippled or waylaid by insensitive remarks their teachers may not even remember saying. We need to recognize that students notice tones of criticism and rejection beyond the words that are said. Conversely, a positive tone and words of encouragement as well as genuine expressions of interest in student ideas and feelings go a long way to encourage and motivate students.

Monitor and Support Engagement

Another aspect of supporting students is noticing how each one participates. Some students have high needs for attention, while others are reticent to raise their hands. When Becki taught first grade, she noticed that Pablo was in perpetual motion and kept calling out. She kept a constant eye on him and managed to call on him about every other time. Some teachers would have considered this unfair to the other students, but Pablo needed extra help in monitoring his behavior. If she had not done this, he still would have been taking class time by misbehaving. This way he became academically engaged and did not disrupt the class nearly as often.

Karen gave feedback privately, and her students clearly felt that she believed they could achieve a particular goal and came to believe in their own abilities. Over the course of the year, shy students came out of their shells, and unsure students gained confidence in new abilities.

Another form of engagement is sharing in activities with the students. When Karen's students read silently, she pulled out her novel. When they did artwork, she often worked on a piece of her own. Melania (Grade 4) modeled how she loved to write, saying,

I was working on writing a children's chapter book at the time, so I brought in chapters, and the students loved critiquing them. Jeanie, a girl from Vietnam, had many good suggestions. She had strong writing skills, and my modeling gave her confidence to share her work, even though she was still mastering English grammar. She felt safe enough to read her pieces to the class, and she asked them to help edit her English. Students did some great pieces of writing that year.

Students who feel connected to their teachers are more likely to engage fully in the curriculum. Through engagement, they start to explore and take risks. When teachers acknowledge their efforts, these explorations lead to a sense of competence, which cycles back into more feelings of success and connection in the classroom.

CHALLENGES AND DILEMMAS

One might think that there would be no dilemmas with regard to trying to be warm and available to students, yet there are. We will explore three dilemmas:

1. nobody is unlovable, or how to be warm when a student is hard to love;

2. how to effectively praise and give feedback; and

3. how to provide support to students who have had repeated failures.

Nobody Is Unlovable

It is totally understandable that a child who continually disrupts the class can be hard to love. It is also normal to like some children more than others. However, the identity safe teacher can challenge herself to find a way to care about each child and draw out hidden qualities. This is more a question of attitude than anything else, followed by taking the time to get to know the child.

Dorothy was frustrated by one of her preschool students who seemed to resist any guidance from her. Darrin found it especially hard to stop one activity and move to another. Returning to the classroom from the play yard was especially hard for Darrin. One day, not without a little frustration, Dorothy stopped to pay attention to what Darrin was doing instead of returning to the classroom. She noticed that he was totally engaged in looking at the plants in the yard and the bugs that inhabited them.

She realized that he had a genuine interest in this, and she was able to provide him with books and a microscope to learn more about nature. She felt a lot less frustrated with him when she saw him as a budding scientist!

Melania noticed that once she made that effort to get to know her fourth grade students, she always found something special about each of them. When one mother shared that her son Juan taught his sister to read, Melania no longer saw him only as the boy who was always picking fights. She found a kindergartener for him to read with, and he rose to the occasion and did a great job. That in turn caused her to feel much better about him, and together they worked on strengthening his impulse control. Finding some way to love each child does not prevent that child from getting on your last nerve, but it is a value and attitude that is transformative both for the child and for your experience of that student in your classroom.

Praise and Feedback

Praise and feedback are not exactly the same thing. Research on the effects of praise offers various insights into ways to effectively praise and provide honest feedback. Students need encouragement, yet feedback should guide them forward in learning and skill building.

The self-esteem movement of the 1970s had far-reaching effects on teachers and parents, causing them to offer voluminous praise while hesitating to correct errors out of fear of damaging a child's self-concept. But, too much praise can create in children a dependence on praise that may, in fact, lower their self-confidence rather than promote their self-esteem. If parents or teachers make too many comments like "good job," it may pump students up but not build students' confidence in their own competence.

Researcher Alfie Kohn (2006) warns against using praise to manage the classroom. For example, a common refrain heard in classrooms is "I like the way Sean is sitting quietly." Such comments can inadvertently cause competition and can backfire into resentment by the other students. Another way to get the same results while promoting self-regulation is to say, "Check yourself and see if you are sitting quietly with your legs crossed." Comments like this help tell students what you want them to do and enable them to be in charge of their own behavior.

Psychologist Carol Dweck (2006) suggests praising effort, rather than intelligence. In Dweck's study, students who were praised for their intelligence did not try to improve their performance and often gave up on challenging tasks, while those praised for effort were more likely to take on and persist with a challenging task. Specific feedback serves as a guide for building skills and can be combined with encouraging words about effort.

How teachers give feedback has important effects on whether students believe the feedback and can use the feedback to try to improve their work. The manner of giving feedback is especially important when the teacher is white and the students belong to a negatively stereotyped group. Because of the negative academic stereotype associated with African American and Latino students, it is especially important that the teacher giving feedback establish a sense of trust between her and the students. In a series of studies, researchers Geoff Cohen, Claude Steele, and Lee Ross (1999) found that teachers who acted "neutral" or began their feedback with some generic praise seemed to raise the suspicions of the students. These students did not believe the feedback and worked less hard at improving their writing assignment. But, when African American students were first told by their teacher that she held high standards and that she believed the students could meet such standards, they accepted the feedback, and they worked even harder than white students to improve their essays when they were given an opportunity to revise them.

When all these ideas are put together, it is evident that teachers need to be intentional when providing feedback and praising students. They need to give specific and clear feedback, praise effort rather than ability, and express confidence in the student's abilities. Students who receive supportive encouragement along the way can learn to reflect on their performance, monitor themselves, and critically analyze their work to prepare for revisions and improved work.

Supporting Students Who Have Experienced Repeated Failures

Harvard psychologist Martin Seligman (2006) found that repeated failures lead to a sense of learned helplessness that results in giving up and even causes illness and depression. Conversely, optimism is also learned (and can be taught) and leads to a willingness to persist and keep trying. These optimistic attitudes can lead to social and academic success as well as physical and mental health. Seligman encourages people to look at the way they explain failures to themselves. He suggests that pessimistic people have three ways they respond to a negative event like a failed test: They might consider it personal—"I am bad at math and must be stupid." Or they might consider it permanent—"I fail every time I take a math test." And they might even consider it pervasive—"Since I keep failing, I will never go to college."

Conversely, people with an optimistic explanatory style will respond to a similar failed math test in a different way. They might look at themselves and ask—"Maybe I didn't study enough, and I need to get a tutor or help in some way?" And they may see it as an obstacle, but not a permanent obstacle—"I will study more next time and can probably do better." And ultimately, they do not see the problem as pervasive—"I am good at other things and can eventually get better at math if I try harder." Teachers can work with students to change their self-attributions and learn how to be optimistic. An identity safe classroom is by its very nature an optimistic place.

PUTTING TEACHER WARMTH AND AVAILABILITY TO SUPPORT LEARNING INTO PRACTICE

An important first step is to reflect on your own experience.

1. How do you build rapport when you meet a new person?

2. How do members of your family build rapport?

3. How did your parents teach you to show feelings?

   Then consider which students might need help in establishing positive relationships with you. Try one or more of the activities below and share your results.

4. Try a quick daily check-in at the beginning or end of each day. One easy way to start is to greet each student as the students enter the classroom at the start of the day. Focus your observation on two students who might benefit the most from this closeness, and document any changes in their behavior. What did you observe?

(Continued)

(Continued)

- Ask about their plans for the day or how the day went, what help they might need, or any concerns they might have about how things are going for them in the classroom. This will provide deeper opportunities to learn about your students' experiences in the classroom and permit them to hear your ideas. These check-ins also promote reflective thinking on the part of students and can help them think about their own behavior and its effect on classroom life. What did you discover?

5. Try instituting a get-to-know-you activity in which each student is the focus for a week. Have the student bring in pictures, artifacts, family members, instruments—anything that reflects who the student is and what the student cares about. You could begin the process by being the first to "present" yourself so that students see you as a person and possibly see similarities between you and them. What did you try? What did you learn from this activity?

Positive Student Relationships   **11**

WHY FOCUS ON POSITIVE STUDENT RELATIONSHIPS?

Peer relationships become increasingly important as students get older and move up the grades in school. Especially when students get older and become interested in dating, their social identities such as race, gender, and religion shape their relationships and may put powerful boundaries on them. Without Positive Student Relationships, classrooms can become a frightening place where students can become aggressive, withdraw, or dread coming to school. In each case, their schoolwork will suffer. To avoid these negative student feelings, the teacher can act as the "CEO" (chief experience officer), the architect of the entire classroom experience, so that the way students relate to one another is not left to chance.

Teachers play a decisive role in facilitating positive relationships among students by setting norms for behavior, teaching relational skills, and orchestrating interaction. To give everyone a sense of belonging, teachers need to ensure that students of all ethnic and language groups get to know one another. Students feel a sense of identity safety when they know what behaviors are expected and that the teacher is aware of social dynamics of the classroom and on the schoolyard.

Set norms so that everyone knows that put-downs, bullying, teasing, and exclusion are not acceptable. While occasional conflict is a natural part of life, teachers can try to handle it calmly and teach students how to pause before reacting, articulate their feelings, and listen to each other as they resolve problems. A student needs to be sure that her teacher will intervene if she is being hurt, bullied, or excluded and will address all problems fairly. But, importantly, it is the creation of an inclusive, productive atmosphere that serves as the basis for the Positive Student Relationships. A classroom that is strong in positive relationships is not just free of conflict; it is filled with opportunities for students to interact in supportive, caring ways. A feeling of identity safety comes from the total experience.

POSITIVE STUDENT RELATIONSHIPS: HOW TO DO IT

Structure the Environment to Promote Positive Relationships

An intentional focus on student relationships begins with knowing which children feel safe and finding ways to foster a sense of belonging for each child. Researcher Ira Lit (2009) found that as early as kindergarten, students of color bussed from a low-income neighborhood into a primarily white affluent community felt isolated and on the fringes. Similarly, Stanford University social psychologists Greg Walton and Geoffrey Cohen (2007) found that African American college students who were in the minority on an elite campus questioned whether they belonged. As part of a study, these students were shown films of African American upperclassmen explaining that they too initially faced similar doubts and overcame them. With the understanding that others surmounted struggles like theirs, the students of color came to believe that they would as well. This improved their sense of belonging at the university as well as their academic achievement during the rest of their time at college.

This research shows us the power of belonging in making classrooms places of inclusion and has implications for all classrooms. First, teachers need to observe carefully to determine if students are feeling unsafe. Ongoing observation and monitoring are necessary, because students may respond to various activities differently. A feeling of identity safety is not a permanent condition, but one that may change, depending on the characteristics of the situation. They also can provide role models and encouragement as they structure situations to ensure students feel included in all aspects of school life.

In elementary school, there are many ways to promote positive student relationships. Ann continually worked to help her second grade students develop positive relationships with each other. From the first day, Ann emphasized that everyone needed to get along and work with everyone in the class. She afforded all students many chances to get to know others whom they would not ordinarily seek out, saying, "Students change desk seats and carpet seats every three weeks."

Another teacher teamed his first grade class with a third grade class to create recess buddies. They sometimes met to do activities together, but they also learned to look after each other on the schoolyard. Some teachers employ reading buddies to create a friendly, trusting relationship so that older students can listen to and read with younger students. Both groups of students improve their reading skills, but importantly, this buddy system creates a love of reading and a sense that everyone at school is a reader.

Provide Opportunities for Intergroup Friendships

Aspects of belonging and positive relationships among students have additional nuances in diverse groups. The underlying assumption in identity safety is that colorblind classrooms are not conducive to belonging. Rather, students in diverse groups need to feel acceptance and belonging in the full composite of their identities. Teachers can be actively involved to ensure that intergroup friendships and relationships are built.

As mentioned above, when Ira Lit (2009) observed African American and Latino kindergarteners bussed from a low-income community to a high-income community, he saw these students often playing alone on the school yard. And when he interviewed them, he found out that they were unsure of how the teachers wanted them to act in the classroom. He saw well-meaning teachers who did not notice that these students felt out of place. He also saw other teachers who did recognize that the students who were bussed to the school may have felt a sense of being different and outside. These teachers greeted the bus every day, giving a message that the bussed students were welcome in the school. In an identity safe classroom, the teacher learns to pay attention to students who are being excluded, creating opportunities for each member to get to know and work with every classmate to form an inclusive community.

For example, one teacher was well aware that her white and Asian kindergarten students lived in the local neighborhood and that the two African American students in her class came to school on the bus. For that reason, she worked with parents at the beginning of the year to develop playgroups, so that no child would miss the opportunity to have play dates and to socialize with their peers in and outside of school.

Monitor Interactions on the Schoolyard

Teachers in an identity safe classroom watch how the students treat one another in class *and* on the schoolyard. Recess and lunch can be extremely unsafe times for students (Lewis, 2003). Ken watched his fourth grade students interact on the schoolyard during recess and lunch, intervening when necessary:

I got involved in what happens on the schoolyard. There's nothing sadder than seeing children on the playground wandering around by themselves when they don't have the tools to make friends.

Melania found out that her fourth grade student Tanya was so frightened that she hid in a bathroom stall for the entire lunch period:

When I discovered that, I was heartsick. From that time forward, I made sure to find out how each child was feeling and provided a chance for children to share experiences that happened outside their classroom, either through formal or informal processes.

She also opened her classroom at lunch and set out some games for students to play together.

Meera (Grade 5) sometimes had to stop her prepared lesson and drop everything:

Sometimes you have planned this great lesson and the kid comes in crying after lunch. If you really need to talk to the kid, you use silent reading time to talk it out. Or if it is the whole class, you just have a discussion. There are times you must say, "Too bad! If I don't get to the reading, I don't get to the reading." I don't want that child going home unhappy with things unresolved. We need to discuss it.

In order to significantly reduce stereotype threat, identity safe teachers address influences outside the classroom door. This may seem like an added duty for a teacher, but the cost of not addressing what is bothering children affects the learning and mood of the class. The good news is that, with this classroom practice, students learn tools for negotiating the world outside the classroom.

Promote Students' Sense of Belonging

In an identity safe classroom, teachers work to create a positive community where all students feel proud to belong. People have a natural tendency to affiliate. Researchers found that a sense of affiliation could be created by something as simple as a shared birthday. College students expressed a greater liking for math when they were told that the professor shared their birthday (Dunning, 2010). Most schools already have spirit week and other activities that capitalize on the natural need to affiliate, but these can also be used to promote school values.

Becki shared,

We created school spirit by identifying the positive caring qualities of our school and our values in the Franklin School pledge. Then to create a college-going mentality and school spirit, each class adopted a university. At the weekly assemblies, one student led the whole school in the pledge, and classes sang their colleges' fight songs. At the end, together we would shout, "We are the Franklin Firebirds on the road to college."

Conversely, peer pressure and inadequate affiliation can create negative behaviors. Teachers need to monitor classroom cliques and dynamics, which can influence not only relationships but also achievement. Even elementary schools have been faced with a growing trend of cyber-bullying, which includes everything from threatening text messages to attacks on Facebook and other social media. One classroom discussed ways to counteract the effects of cyber-bullying. They came up with a campaign to put positive messages on Facebook. This effort was made into a short film to share with other schools, and their campaign spread like wildfire, continuing beyond the duration of their class project (O'Neill, 2011).

According to Greg Walton and Geoff Cohen, social belonging has a powerful influence over everyone's life. The need for belonging influences every aspect of our identities, including attitudes, motivation, and achievement. These aspects of our identities are shaped by the attitudes, motivations, and achievement of people who are most important to us.

Teachers create a sense of belonging when they are conscious of group dynamics and intervene when necessary. A classroom can become a safe home base for the students, where everyone's feelings are considered and the teacher facilitates students' sense of belonging by expressly stating the importance of belonging as the foundation of school norms. Support for students' sense of belonging must also be upheld in practice, as seen in the next examples.

Resolve Problems and Conflicts

A variety of conflict resolution methodologies are available that break down the steps for solving disagreements. Each model includes the same basic ingredients: respectful listening, understanding each other's perspectives, and arriving at mutually acceptable resolutions. The elements of the process include teaching the students to listen to one another, to ask for what they need, and to find a solution that is acceptable to all parties. Becki recalls what her school did to solve conflicts using this approach:

In nearly all cases, this type of resolution ended the problem. Substitutes used to enter our large urban school and marvel "The students seem so calm here; what is different about this school?" I knew it was because all teachers worked together to implement a combination of the character education program that we used to create norms for positive interaction and our conflict resolution program that guided students in solving their differences.

In her second grade classroom, Ann took the conflict resolution process one step further, helping students rebuild broken relationships: "After they solve the conflict, I remind them that we all have to be in class all year long, so I send them on a little walk. They love it and all come back holding hands." In an identity safe classroom, teachers help students learn how to de-escalate conflicts and resolve them when they occur. With teachers' help, students can repair broken relationships and use their new skills to mitigate future conflicts.

Sometimes the incident is not a conflict but a stereotyping remark. When she was a principal, Becki observed a beginning teacher:

> During a group discussion in a new teacher's sixth grade classroom, one girl said to a classmate "That's so gay." The teacher said nothing. Later, I pointed out to this teacher it is always important to address any type of name calling. When he brought it up to the class for discussion, the girl said that she meant nothing by the comment; it just means that's so weird.
>
> Another student said, "If you mean 'that's so weird,' why don't you just say that? What you said does put down all gay people."

Although the original teachable moment went by, it is never too late to address comments that affect students. When teachers do not intervene, we give the message that such comments are acceptable. We can teach the students how to speak up when they hear stereotypical comments when we model how to intervene.

Respond to Bullying

The basic need for belonging is a powerful force and a double-edged sword that can move people to both positive and negative acts to seek approval. Students seeking to belong or to move up the social ladder may engage in acts of social cruelty, believing that this will increase their status. In the last few years, media coverage of the devastating results of bullying has led to national awareness of the serious need to address unsafe school environments. As a result, there is new antibullying legislation in 49 states.

The entire school community can learn to identify bullying and intolerance. The generally accepted definition of *bullying* is a repeated act of verbal, electronic, or physical aggression with an imbalance of power between the perpetrator and victim. An imbalance of power may be physical strength, access to embarrassing information, or popularity, which is used to try to control, harm, and exclude others.

Intolerance includes unkind remarks with stereotypical comments regarding a person's social identity (race, ethnicity, language, sexual orientation, religion, disability, etc.). Both bullying and intolerance can happen overtly in the classroom, but often they occur out of adult view in the yard or on the bus. In an identity safe environment, *all* acts of bullying and intolerance and *all* forms of social cruelty are addressed to support the victim and to help the perpetrator learn more compassionate ways to behave.

Bystanders can learn to become "upstanders," those who speak up when someone is being hurt. Rather than gathering around when someone is being bullied or spreading a video or text as if it were entertainment, students can reject acts of aggression and cruelty. Positive behaviors, like negative behaviors, are contagious and can spread through social networks (Faris & Felmlee, 2011).

Bullying is handled differently than conflicts among peers in nonbullying situations. Assessing the imbalance of power, adults work with the perpetrator and the target of bullying separately to ensure the target does not feel threatened during or after intervention. We refrain from use of the terms *bully* or *victim* to avoid labeling students and making these negative stereotypes part of the students' identity. Students can also role-play refusal skills to develop confidence in standing up for themselves (Frey et al., 2005).

While identity safe educators give consequences for bullying in accordance with school policy, they also help the perpetrator learn ways to change his behavior. For example, *restorative justice* is a process that provides avenues for students who have harmed others to give back to the community. (For a description of restorative justice, see Chapter 12.)

Becki described how John, who was larger than his fourth grade peers, bullied Samuel, warning that "things will be worse for you if you tell." As a result, Samuel was refusing to go to school. When confronted, John was remorseful, but in spite of being disciplined, he bullied again. When asked to find a solution, John suggested that he could spend recess and lunch volunteering in the preschool. There, he read and played with children; he was always gentle and loved by them. Eventually, John asked if he could go out to recess again with his peers. Yet, after a few better weeks, he "forgot" and bullied again and was sent back to the preschool for more community service. For John, leaving behind his tendency to bully required many parent meetings and sessions with the school counselor. That repeated effort was well worth it, and John slowly began to change.

An identity safe teacher understands the harm of name calling and negative stereotypes and addresses large and small acts of aggression to make school safe for students of all backgrounds and social identities. In identity safe classrooms, the entire climate serves as an antidote to bullying. Inclusion and acceptance are community values, and the positive culture can decrease the incidence of bullying. But when bullying happens, it is immediately addressed, and students are reminded of the classroom norms.

CHALLENGES AND DILEMMAS

As teachers know, there are myriads of challenges and dilemmas in building positive student relationships. We have selected four to examine:

1. deciding when to intervene;

2. determining what to do when a disability affects a student's capacity to be empathetic;

3. determining when to protect student feelings; and

4. the hazards of complimenting during circle time.

Determining When to Intervene

Decisions about when to intervene are often made in the moment. When teachers witness negative interactions that may lead to hurt feelings and anger, they are faced with deciding how much to be involved to help the students work things out. Sometimes teachers have the chance to consider the best way to address a bad social situation and orchestrate an intervention.

For example, Karen addressed both spoken and unspoken feelings when a student was left out or teased. She felt it was incumbent on teachers to intervene to guide students to develop relationships of equitable status. Yet she did not do this by lecturing about positive values. As an example, she told about an African American student, Nelda, from a low-income family, who felt stigmatized after having behavioral troubles at school. Karen invited Nelda to join her and several students for a special lunch in her classroom. Karen did this to facilitate her connection with the students and their connection with one another. During their lunch, the students talked about their lives and discussed the chores they did at home. In the process, the other fifth grade girls became aware of and were quite amazed at the level of independence and responsibility that Nelda shouldered. Karen was impressed, because she valued Nelda's practical abilities, which outshined those of a typical child her age. Karen felt that this was a turning point for Nelda; the children talking about their home lives at lunch raised Nelda's status in her classroom. Karen felt that Nelda's newfound status and sense of belonging contributed to an overall improvement in Nelda's performance.

This example highlights the power of positive relationships in the classroom. However, it also highlights the highly subjective elements that equalize status. Perhaps having a student share that she does extra chores does not, in itself, necessarily guarantee increased status within a society that holds an inferior view of people who perform manual labor. Yet, in this case, the teacher mediated the situation, and the results were transformative.

What to Do When a Disability Affects a Student's Capacity to Be Empathetic

At times, student insensitivity is the result of particular disabilities that influence behavior. Students with ADHD have a lack of impulse control and can react suddenly, before they consider the affect of their behavior. Some students on the autism spectrum have an inability to read body language and understand another person's emotions. These situations require understanding the way the disability impacts empathy, followed by explicit teaching, careful monitoring, and lots of patience. Though a student's poor behavior can be explained by a disability, the misbehavior can have a negative influence on the student who is the recipient of a hurtful comment or aggressive action. In Ann's class, Josh, a student with Asperger syndrome, compromised a sense of belonging for his classmate, an English learner who was just learning to read:

> Mara read word by word, and Josh began to shout, "You're so stupid, you read like you're in preschool, you don't even know how to read the words." And this girl had worked so hard.

This was particularly difficult because Ann had been trying to build up Mara's reading skills and self-esteem. She needed to teach social skills to Josh while continuing to build Mara's confidence. At first Ann felt overwhelmed by this dilemma. Her solution was to approach the issue on several levels. She worked with Josh individually to help him to improve his social skills. She went to the school speech and language therapist who used Social Stories (http://www.thegraycenter.org/social-stories), specific scenarios designed to teach Josh how to identify feelings, read facial expressions, and respond to social cues. Ann reinforced Josh's new learning about the difference between saying nice and mean things to others. Ann recognized this was a process that would not happen instantly.

To Mara she explained privately that she was sorry Josh said such a hurtful thing and assured her that Josh was completely wrong. She helped Mara see her own improvement in reading. She explained that Josh had his own area to work on too, that of not saying hurtful things.

This incident also highlights the importance of promoting equal status among students who function at different academic levels, whether or not they have disabilities.

Determine When to Protect Student Feelings

Another challenge involves understanding that a teacher cannot always stop a student's feelings from being hurt. And it can be difficult to know when it is best to let students resolve issues without teacher intervention. In identity safe classrooms, teachers regularly monitor when students are upset and encourage them to tell the teacher if they feel left out or uncomfortable. The IDS study group (author Becki Cohn-Vargas's identity safety study group) discussed that no teacher or parent could or should *always* protect students from difficult situations. Part of becoming resilient is learning to bounce back and forgive after having hurt feelings. Optimism can be learned, and teachers both model and help students learn to deal with uncomfortable feelings and setbacks.

The Hazards of Circle Time Focused on Student Compliments

Complimenting is a useful social skill that can strengthen kindness and appreciation for one another and contributes to a positive climate by having everyone looking for good. Many teachers have students compliment one another during circle time. While this activity may appear to have a positive effect on the students, it runs the risk of strengthening in-groups and reinforcing out-groups, as certain students compliment only their friends.

For example, in Meera's class, Saul sat on the edge of his seat waiting to hear what the other boys said during circle time. When Peter started complimenting his friends and did not mention Saul, Saul's face fell. Meera realized that the popular boys complimented each other frequently and that this well-intentioned circle activity served to reinforce unequal status in her classroom. She decided that this method needed to change to help students appreciate others who might not be in their social circle.

Karen shared how she handled complimenting among students. She did not encourage general complimenting among students. Rather, after student presentations, she instructed students to share a positive observation with a partner next to them in the circle. Then she randomly drew a name and selected someone to share his or her thoughts with the class. This allowed all students to hear positive comments and taught them to search for good things to say about everyone's work.

PUTTING POSITIVE STUDENT RELATIONSHIPS INTO PRACTICE

Try one of these ideas or others you know to promote positive relationships in your classroom.

1. Take time at the beginning of the year to play some "get to know you" games such as this:
   • Have students stand in one line facing the teacher or one student leader. Pose various questions such as, Who has a pet dog? or, Who loves to jump rope or play basketball? or, Who plays a musical instrument? When students say "I do" to any of these questions, they cross the room and become a part of a subgroup of the class. Teachers can invite students to elaborate on their answers or to observe who is in the subgroup with them. Membership in any of these subgroups can provide later grouping for working on some academic task or clean-up team or anything that builds on the students' shared interests. There are no stakes involved, and these subgroups are just a way to help students "see" one another and appreciate shared interests. These would be, of course, very temporary groups. How would this activity work with your students?

2. Encourage helping.
    • Teachers can encourage students to help one another in both spontaneous and planned ways. Helping also conveys empathy and shows respect for one another. How can you encourage helping in your class without formalizing it, so that students spontaneously help one another?

3. Express empathy.
    • Assist your students in writing a get-well or sympathy card for a classmate who has a prolonged illness or who has lost someone important.

Part IV Summary

Teachers play the major role, as "chief experience officers," in orchestrating positive relationships at school. They combine their warmth and caring with making themselves available to all students and giving help and encouragement for both social and academic efforts. By focusing attention on the social dynamics of the classroom—such as who speaks up, who is chosen to participate in various activities, which students have friends, and who does not— teachers can adjust classroom arrangements, activities, and groupings to address social problems that can become barriers to students' learning.

Spending time helping students get to know one another or learn to help one another can seem like a luxury under the press of time teachers feel for covering all the academic work that they are expected to present to students. But, because of the social nature of learning and the need for belonging that all students have, the small time it takes to engage students in conversations about their interests, knowledge, or unseen skills, or in teaching them to work together, should pay off over and over during the school year.

Though social interactions are bound to bring with them conflicts, challenges, and dilemmas, by paying close attention to student relationships and maintaining strong relationships with each student, teachers can use these situations as learning opportunities. As teachers watch to ensure that students are not publically embarrassed or humiliated or put in competition with one another, students come to feel a sense of fairness and safety that calms fears and gives them confidence. Finally, teachers can work to create inclusive, noncolorblind classrooms by using materials, representations, languages, and teaching assignments that reflect the cultures, histories, and lived experiences of their students. By implementing these ongoing practices and being willing to address stereotyping and name calling, teachers can make the classroom identity safe for all students.

Part IV References

Cohen, G. L., Steele, C. M., & Ross, L. D. (1999). The mentor's dilemma: Providing critical feedback across the racial divide. *Personality and Social Psychology Bulletin, 25,* 1302–1310.

Dunning, D. (2010). *Social motivation.* New York, NY: Psychology Press.

Dweck, C. (2006). *Mindset.* New York, NY: Random House.

Faris, R., & Felmlee, D. (2011). Status struggles: Network centrality and gender segregation in same- and cross-gender aggression. *American Sociological Review, 76*(1), 48–73.

Frey, K. S., Hirschstein, M. K., Snell, J. L., Edstrom, L. V., MacKenzie, E. P., & Broderick, C. J. (2005). Reducing playground bullying and supporting beliefs: An experimental trial of the *Steps to Respect* program. *Developmental Psychology, 41*(3), 479–491.

Goleman, D. (2006). *Social intelligence.* New York, NY: Bantam.

Kohn, A. (1996). *Beyond discipline: From compliance to community.* Alexandria VA: ASCD.

Lewis, A. E. (2003). *Race in the schoolyard: Negotiating the color line in classrooms and communities.* New Brunswick, NJ: Rutgers University Press.

Lit, I. (2009). *The bus kids: Children's experiences with voluntary desegregation.* New Haven, CT: Yale University Press.

O'Neill, P. (Director). (2011). *Not in our town: Light in the darkness* [Motion picture]. Oakland, CA: The Working Group. Available from NIOT.org

Seligman, M. (2006). *Learned optimism: How to change your mind and your life.* New York, NY: Vintage Books.

Steele, C. M. (2010). *Whistling Vivaldi: And other clues to how stereotypes affect us.* New York, NY: W. W. Norton.

Takimoto, L. (2006). *Focused identity safety* (Unpublished master's thesis). School of Education, Saint Mary's College of California, Moraga, CA.

Walton, G. M., & Cohen, G. L. (2007). A question of belonging: Race, social fit, and achievement. *Journal of Personality and Social Psychology, 92,* 82–96.

Part V

Caring Classrooms

WHAT DO WE MEAN BY CARING CLASSROOMS?

Many new teachers have been advised to base their classroom management on the old adage, "Don't smile until Christmas." The problem with this approach to designing the classroom environment is that not smiling sets up a top-down relationship between teachers and students. Instead of showing respect and caring toward the students, it creates a "my way or the highway" atmosphere that does not demonstrate concern for how the students experience life in the classroom. This approach controls students, rather than engaging them as participating members of the class. And, this approach does not teach students to consider how their behavior affects the classroom or give them responsibility for their own behavior.

But other teachers realize that strict discipline and punishment do not form the basis for a successful, well-managed class. Instead, teachers who want students to learn interpersonal skills based on awareness of themselves and others will focus on creating caring environments that foster self-discipline and opportunities for students to learn interpersonal skills and think about how their behavior affects themselves and others. This focus helps teachers create a sense of identity safety for everyone in the classroom.

Our Stanford Integrated Schools Project (SISP) study found that three factors, taken together, help to create caring classroom environments. These factors, much like the water a fish swims in or the air we breathe, form the backdrop for all teachers' efforts to create an identity safe classroom.

A definition of each of the three factors follows.

Teacher Skill includes all aspects of a well-managed classroom focused on *engaging* rather than *controlling* students. Each aspect of the classroom's physical setup and procedures is thought out carefully to anticipate difficult situations and moments, prevent behavior problems, and ensure smooth transitions.

Emotional and Physical Comfort work together in creating an identity safe classroom. Emotional Comfort is the result of teachers helping to set a tone that is neither hectic and frenetic nor tense and pressured. Instead, students feel more identity safe because their teacher creates a relaxed and pleasant atmosphere. Students are free to engage informally with the teacher and one another, creating a sense of community. The mood is friendly, unhurried, and supportive, allowing the students to feel emotionally safe and protected, even in the eventuality that things go wrong. The focus is on showing all students that they are accepted and included as valued members of the classroom community.

Physical Comfort includes having needed materials, space to move around, and an appealing classroom with a home-like feeling. In a comfortable workspace, students are able to collaborate in small and large groups and easily shift to quiet reading and independent work. Displaying the work of all students, whether it is perfect or not, will help students recognize that persistence and revisions are the path to improvement. Music, photos, artwork, plants, and even animals enhance the homey feeling. Organized, welcoming environments create a sense of both emotional and physical comfort.

Attention to Prosocial Development is often set aside or ignored with the pressure to improve achievement. Yet, just as students need to be taught reading, writing, and arithmetic, they need to learn and practice respect, empathy, listening, and responsibility as part of daily interactions.

Through class meetings and lessons focused on nonacademic issues, they can explore and practice social skills focused on real interactions among students in the classroom. During academic instruction, students can use these social skills and reflect on how they work together in partners and small groups. Time devoted to teaching interpersonal skills goes a long way to improve student interactions, ultimately saving time spent in solving conflicts. *How they live together* at school is just as important to their overall success as *what they learn.*

Teacher Skill   **12**

WHY TEACHER SKILL?

Teacher Skill refers to the capacity to "plan a purposeful classroom where transitions are clear and smooth, provide an orderly focused classroom, and prevent behavior problems by anticipating difficult situations and redirecting. Teachers focus on engaging students rather than 'controlling' them" (Steele, D. M., 2012, p. 1127). The teacher is the architect of an environment that integrates strong, positive relationships with high expectations and rigorous curriculum to engage and stretch the students. Curriculum and instruction tailored to the students' backgrounds and experiences is designed to appeal to their interests, so they can relate to the content and build on their own knowledge. Teacher Skill in an identity safe environment features a combination of skillful instructional strategies and thoughtful management systems in a warm, culturally sensitive environment.

Teacher Skill includes the basic aspects of teaching, such as procedures for all classroom functions and a series of well-planned lessons with smooth transitions. Teacher Skill is a crucial component in the constellation of identity safety factors. It includes how the environment is designed to facilitate students' learning to manage their behavior. It is how instruction is delivered to engage students in their learning. Many of the aspects of Teacher Skill are learned during teacher preparation and will seem familiar. Yet, Teacher Skill as a factor is highlighted, because identity safety will not happen in a chaotic classroom environment or when more time is spent on punitive discipline than on teaching. It also does not happen when students feel disregarded or fear their teacher or their peers. These skills will grow with experience and time, and, as with students, success breeds more success.

TEACHER SKILL: HOW TO DO IT

The Science and Art of Teaching

In an identity safe classroom, the teacher learns to identify and design lessons to draw on each student's unique capabilities and interests. As an integral part of instruction, she teaches students how to plan, organize, complete their work, and how to seek help when they need it. The teacher also makes sure there are no hidden rules that may be understood by some but prevent others from succeeding. While some students absorb new information like sponges and need to be set free to figure things out for themselves, others struggle to keep up. The *science of teaching* is providing certain students with more explicit strategies that break content down into discrete steps, while providing the correct level of challenge for everyone. Knowing who needs what and finding innovative ways to provide for the different needs is the *art of teaching.*

Maintaining a comfortable environment does not preclude holding students to high expectations. It is delicate balance between creating a comfortable, relaxed atmosphere and one that promotes rigor. A teacher may inadvertently make students a little too comfortable and not challenge them. Conversely, a teacher who wants to raise the bar on expectations may pressure the class so much that students do not feel they can meet the expectations and ultimately give up. Given the varied academic levels and needs in every classroom, teachers create scaffolds for learning so that it is safe to learn from mistakes. Teachers can provide scaffolding by having students work together to help one another, by reteaching in small groups, and by focusing on student mistakes as opportunities for learning rather than moments of failure. A goal of Teacher Skill is to combine rigor and high expectations in a warm and motivating atmosphere.

Becki reported,

> A teacher told me that, though he teaches to the standards, too many students were getting Ds and Fs on their work. He was looking for strategies to ensure he was not sailing through the standards while leaving large numbers of students behind. He began giving more pretests to see what learning gaps needed to be filled to meet grade level standards. He explored offering more scaffolds through small group teaching sessions. He also offered reteaching sessions, allowing students to prepare to retake tests.

The variability in students' levels of accomplishment makes it difficult for teachers, because they must cover vast swaths of the material by standardized testing time. Yet, observing students' behavior and level of success with every learning activity will help teachers meet the students where they are, not where they think the students should be.

Set Up the Environment for Success

When the environment is set up for success, students help themselves, and teachers spend less time directly controlling them. Using indirect methods, teachers can limit unwanted behaviors and encourage positive interactions. For example, a strategy as simple as putting pieces of tape on the rug—for first graders to sit on so they avoid bunching up—sets up the environment to make sure that expectations are appropriate for the students' age and developmental level.

In another example, Melania kept lessons short and engaging for her fourth grade students. After an activity that required concentration and sitting, they had a motivating kinesthetic activity. She had a noise thermometer on the wall to indicate the acceptable noise level for each activity. She always provided additional lessons for students who finished work ahead of the others, and students knew where to find the materials.

In a classroom with indirect control, the goal is for teacher management to become less obvious as students are able to manage themselves. The activities flow, and the mood is upbeat. Underneath this apparently natural structure are careful planning and the teacher's hard work anticipating student needs.

Define Clear and Reasonable Expectations and Procedures

As Becki described her first hellish year as a first grade teacher, she reflected on how she was constantly correcting student behavior and repeating herself like a broken record:

> Luckily, that year I attended a lecture that transformed how I managed my classroom. The speaker emphasized how often students misbehave not because they want to be disruptive, but because they either do not know or do not understand expected behaviors, or the classroom procedures are not consistent.

The lectures helped Becki realize that she needed to spend more time teaching students basic classroom routines and practicing them. She made the process fun, teaching students procedures for everything from sharpening a pencil to lining up for lunch. She even found a solution to the problem that students often interrupted the lesson to ask to go to the bathroom. She asked the students to help design a simple sign-out system:

At first, I worried that first graders might not be able to handle this level of responsibility. So, to begin, I explained the reasons for creating a new system. I told them that too much class time was taken up if we stopped every time someone needed to go to the bathroom. Since it was right across the hall, I told them I was confident that they were mature enough to go on their own. Together we set guidelines, such as don't play with water and walk quietly to and from the bathroom. We went over each of the steps and then role-played the whole process, practicing how to sign out, to leave, and upon return, to erase their names. They loved role-playing, and I found this system not only minimized the interruptions but also increased their sense of autonomy and responsibility.

For each procedure, she modeled, they practiced, and once they were able to do it independently, the class evaluated themselves. As they continued to improve and master the procedures, she praised them, and they took pride in simple accomplishments. "Now, before I assume a student is misbehaving because he wants to cause trouble, I check to see if he knows the procedure."

Linda found that even sixth graders need explicit teaching about things they had done for years, like raising a hand to ask a question or good ways to participate in class discussion.

Getting them engaged was hard at times, but necessary, and ultimately the key to their learning and progress. Part of getting the students engaged was explicitly teaching them what engagement might look, sound, and feel like: sitting up at the desk, taking notes, completing and sharing work, and asking questions about the work. I also taught them to look directly at anyone speaking and how to turn toward a partner for a pair-share.

Linda helped her students reflect on how they performed the expected behaviors. She found that her lessons went more smoothly when she explicitly reviewed these behaviors and gave her students time to consider their own behavior. She felt that this approach to classroom management left her less tired at the end of the day.

Engage Every Child at Least Once Every 10 Minutes

Student engagement is the bridge between teaching and learning, ensuring that what is taught is both learned and retained (Wolfe, 1998). Students need to actively interact with the content through frequent and varied strategies. Engagement can happen in graphic, written, or verbal form. It also can happen in the student's minds when teachers give them time to visualize or think about an idea.

A rule of thumb is to actively engage students at least once every 10 minutes during instruction. Some teachers ask students to quickly turn to a partner and restate the definition or concept in their own words. At other times, students are asked to jot down three ideas or solve a problem on small white boards at their desks. Hand signals can be used to quickly poll for opinions or to check for understanding. When teachers ask students to imagine or visualize something, they follow up by posing a question and providing think time. These engagement strategies ensure that all students are engaged during the entire lesson and give students a chance to get help immediately if they don't understand.

Solving Problems

Melania found that after lunch and recess, her fourth grade students regularly came to her with all the small and large conflicts that happened on the yard. Her solution was to hold class meetings to solve problems daily after lunch. When a problem occurred in class or during recess, either the teacher or a student wrote the problem on an agenda, and during the class meeting, Melania and her students worked together to find solutions.

Staff and students at Karen's school used one of the many conflict resolution models for problem solving. They learned that conflict is a natural part of social interactions and were taught tools for listening to each other and asking for what they needed. Students took turns serving as "conflict managers." Students with nonphysical conflicts went to the assigned managers, who worked in pairs and followed the process they learned during training. They began by asking everyone involved in the conflict a sequence of questions such as, "What happened? How did you feel? What did you do in response? What did the other child do? What do you need to be able to solve the problem?" Karen reported that one of the parents was worried that having students help solve each other's conflicts would lead to fighting. Karen assured that parent that the students were taught to find an adult immediately if there was a physical altercation or an escalation. These adults would meet separately with the students involved in a physical conflict. This model, used consistently for many years, resulted in a calm schoolyard.

Karen also taught her fifth grade students how to use "I" language— a way to speak to one another that did not blame the other person or enflame the situation:

We practiced how to say "I feel _____ when _____ happens because I _____, so will you please _____." At first the "I" messages sounded stilted and funny, but with practice the students learned how to not blame one another and to solve problems by expressing their needs. Most of the time, after listening to each other and going through the resolution process, the students didn't need anything else to solve the problem.

The students were proud of their skills. One child said that once, when her parents had an argument, she taught them how to use "I" messages.

Intervening

Despite all the best preventative measures, teachers have moments when they need to intervene. When intervention is needed, identity safe teachers mentally scroll through a set of questions to determine how to respond in relation to the cause of the behavior. For example, Marilyn Watson, in her book *Learning to Trust: Transforming Difficult Elementary Classrooms Through Developmental Discipline* (2003), suggests teachers carefully consider these possibilities before responding to student behaviors:

- Was it unintentional?
- Was it a lack of knowledge of classroom expectations?
- Was it due to a lack of skills?
- Was the student seeking attention?
- Was it due to a lack of impulse control, or anger and rebellion?

Based on the answer, the teacher can determine how to respond effectively.

If the behavior is frequently disruptive or rebellious, the teacher adds another set of questions and adjusts solutions accordingly.

- What is her relationship with the student? Should she carve out special time to spend with the student or give her special responsibilities? The purpose is to help the child feel like she belongs to the classroom community as she learns more appropriate, effective behavior.
- Does the child feel isolated from the others? If so, adjusting seating groupings, or finding another student to be her buddy, can help.
- Is the child experiencing frustration from failure and lack of competence? The teacher can work with the student to find and validate different learning activities or tasks to build success for this child.

- Does the child have enough autonomy? Finding ways for the child to help the class or do things on her own can help build independence and the pride that comes from being responsible.

Taking time to consider why a student behaves in a certain way helps the teacher match the intervention to student needs. For simple mistakes, the teacher uses a reminder for the expected behavior or reteaches the skill. If students are seeking attention or lack impulse control, a longer process includes teaching them to identify when they are likely to react, how to pause, and how to make an appropriate choice. Bullying needs to be handled differently from other conflicts, because it stems from an imbalance of power that can be very complex. You can find an exploration of how to handle bullying in the classroom in Part IV of this book, Classroom Relationships.

It is important to find out whether students hear different messages about behavior at home. Some children have been taught to hit back. In that case, it is important to explain that the school has rules to protect all children. Instead of hitting back, they need to tell an adult. In that way, teachers can assure children that they will be protected, and they can differentiate between what is done at school and what is done at home or on the street without invalidating the directives of the student's family.

If students repeatedly act out due to anger and alienation, they need to be stopped and given reasonable and expected consequences. The consequences are applied with the goal of helping them learn how to behave. The teacher also seeks the causes for the anger to find the root of the problem, sometimes with the help of a school counselor. It will take time and lots of practice for angry students to learn to control themselves.

Use Consequences That Teach Rather Than Punish

In classrooms where students feel a sense of belonging, their behavior is more likely to be positive than in classrooms where top-down authority and punishment rule. For the most part, all students want to behave appropriately, to be accepted, and to feel included. The assumption is that when students feel included in a positive way, they will not want to resist or rebel and will want to contribute to their own success and that of others. But, behavioral problems do occur. The goal in identity safe classrooms is to focus on teaching students rather than punishing them. When problems occur, the teacher can work closely with the student to identify specific steps to remedy the situation.

Remind children that they are constantly faced with choices and need to consider whether their choices are safe and appropriate. Unsafe behaviors that hurt others, blatant defiance of the teacher, and major disruption to learning are choices that are not acceptable in the classroom. Teachers can help students learn to make appropriate and positive choices.

Communicating respectfully and firmly with students allows them to take responsibility for mistakes without feeling humiliated or shamed. When students are asked to reflect on their actions, they are more likely to learn from the consequences of their behavior. They can also be asked to propose a consequence that will help them learn not to repeat the behavior.

A reasonable consequence for disruption is to change the proximity of the student to the teacher by temporarily or permanently changing seats. A logical consequence for not completing work is to complete it at another time, even if that takes the child away from a preferred activity. Teachers may need to remove a student from the classroom or involve the principal, but this type of intervention should be used only for more serious or frequently repeated infractions.

Teachers and administrators can work together to find alternatives to removal or suspension, in the effort to avoid it as much as possible. In looking for alternatives, they may consider questions such as, "Is this a repeating pattern for the student?" "What are we doing to get at the root of the problem?" Though removal or suspension can serve as a learning opportunity when accompanied with dialogue, reflection, and complete inclusion when the student returns, it should be used when other strategies have failed to help students control their behaviors.

An identity safe approach to serious or frequent misbehavior is to help the student realize that the teacher respects her, and that it is her behavior, not herself as a person, that is causing the problems. With firm and empathetic private pep talks from her teacher, such a student can actively participate in finding ways to improve her behavior. It helps to involve the parents, but they, too, will need to learn what the objectives and desired outcomes are for a student who has been in trouble.

Becki described the importance of including parents:

I love working closely with the parents, because I know they want their children to be successful. With so many different cultures in our school, we make sure to talk with parents and caregivers about school policies and practices that may be different from what they have always done.

Restorative Justice, a Consequence That Restores Dignity

A remedy for hurting or harming others is to make up for it by giving something back to the community. Teachers can determine day-to-day consequences based on this principle. *Restorative justice* is a structured model to help students with serious behavior problems make amends for the harm they have done by shifting from hurting the community to helping the community. The goal of restorative justice is to help students with major discipline problems transform their negative behavior and become resilient and contributing members of the school community. As an additional benefit, restorative justice helps teachers see disruptive students' strengths, which get dwarfed when their teachers are continually dealing with the students' daily infractions. When teachers find they cannot think of anything positive about a child, the first step is to strengthen their relationship with the student.

The restorative justice process in schools focuses on the student reflecting deeply on the harm he has caused as well as thinking about the strengths he can use to remedy the situation. It involves repairing harm through community service as an alternative to suspension, followed by support to maintain new behaviors. For elementary school students, the process could include members of the school community such as the librarian who always needs help organizing books, the school secretary who has errands to run, or lunch supervisors who need help cleaning tables. This approach strengthens the sense of community, as students, faculty, and staff participate in creating a sense of security where mistakes can be repaired and forgiven. This process helps all involved to feel pride in each child's transformation (Braithwaite, 2000).

For example, one principal used the process to support Lamar, whose repeated aggressive acts came to a climax when he purposefully knocked a disabled girl off her crutches. The process involved making it clear to him that his behavior was unacceptable, identifying his strengths, and helping him find what he could do to repair the harm by helping someone else. As a result Lamar became a volunteer in a class for students who were physically and mentally disabled. He turned out to be a gentle and kind helper and as a result transformed how he saw himself and how he behaved.

CHALLENGES AND DILEMMAS

We will touch on three major challenges to implementing Teacher Skill:

1. finding time to guide student behavior in the middle of a lesson,

2. maintaining teacher authority without humiliating students, and

3. using intrinsic rather than extrinsic motivators to get students to comply.

Finding Time to Resolve an Issue

Teachers are always faced with a time dilemma when behavior problems interrupt classroom instruction. They have several options. When a serious incident occurs, a teacher can stop everything and address it, especially when the whole group is upset and it is unlikely they could focus on learning anyway. In contrast, for less pressing incidents, teachers can address the issue quickly in the moment and come back to it later. That gives time for the teacher to consider the best response and also give the students a cool-off period.

Meera described an incident that happened when she had no time to completely address the issue. She decided to make it a teachable moment and then returned later for a fuller discussion. The conversation began as a typical discussion during circle time, where Meera introduced an important concept, common sense:

> I asked, "What does it mean to have common sense?" The students were all giving their opinions of what common sense means and why it's important. For example, if you don't have common sense, you might put your hand into boiling water. . . . It's your common sense that prevents you from doing things like that.
>
> One student said, "Having common sense means not going to play in a park late at night in Peralta." I was quiet for a minute. I thought of Jaime, who gets bussed from Peralta, a low-income area, near to this school, where most of the students are much more affluent. How do I take care of this? So I said, "Why Peralta?" And the girl said, "Well, you know, it's dangerous in Peralta."

Meera looked over at Jaime and saw he was sitting all curled up with his head down. She realized that she could not just let the conversation follow its course without guidance. She thought about the fact that the girl had used a negative stereotype of a neighboring community, making Jaime feel ashamed and excluded. Meera continued,

> That's stereotyping, you know; that's what you've heard. Is it okay to go to a park in Flora Linda late at night?
>
> The girl said, "No."
>
> So I said, "Any place can be dangerous. So why choose a community, Peralta?"
>
> So then somebody else said, "Oh, yeah, Oakland, too!"

When Meera's students offered more stereotypes, she realized they did not get her point:

So that was an unexpected response again. I thought somebody was going to say, "Oh yeah, it can happen in our neighborhood, too." I was waiting for that. Well, it came to Oakland. At that point I said, "It's stereotyping, and it could happen in a park next door. It could be across the street in the park. Going out alone late at night is not using common sense in any place. It doesn't have to be Peralta or Oakland."

Meera realized that she needed more time than she had right then to address the idea of stereotyping, which her fifth grade students did not yet understand. She also realized that she needed to listen to their views in order to engage with them:

Then I needed to move on, but we brought that topic up later in the day, again, because I didn't want to let it drop. I wanted the kids to understand why I had said "not just Peralta." I asked them what guides their views. "Oh, because in the papers, we keep hearing how there's drive-by shootings in Peralta."

I said, "Shootings happen in our town, too. Something happened in my neighborhood, too, and it was shut down. This can happen anywhere, where people sometimes do not use common sense and do things that are not appropriate. We have kids here who come from Peralta. They live in that community. Really, 99% of the people are good people, anywhere in the world. You need to see that first before you see the negative in people."

Later, Jaime went up to the girl who made the comment and said, "See?" He just kind of gave her that big look. "See? It's not just my community, so don't be saying that. It happens everywhere."

Meera was not willing to let the stereotypical comment stand unchecked. She listened to her students to understand their thinking in order to provide them with another perspective. She noted that Jaime, though he said little at first, was listening intently. He later told her that he appreciated her intervention on behalf of his town.

This incident also pointed to the difficult realities and choices facing a teacher. That year Peralta had an increase in drive-by shootings, events that threatened to increase the stereotype threat in the classroom and to stigmatize individual students. Meera was faced with finding a way to respond without further stigmatizing Jaime. She was able to respond thoughtfully and without singling him out. She handled the situation briefly in the moment and more in-depth by returning to the topic of stereotypes later.

Responding With Authority Without Humiliating Students

Is it possible to validate a child's sense of self even when a serious incident has occurred? At one school where she was the principal, Becki handled a seriously dangerous situation when sixth grade girls lit matches in the bathroom and started a small fire. Luckily, the fire did not spread, but instead of reporting it, the girls hurried out to avoid being detected. After investigating to learn who did it, Becki brought the girls into her office. Her tone was firm and her words were respectful, but by the end, the students knew that by starting the fire, they put everyone in the school at risk. Yet, even in this extremely dangerous situation, she was careful not to shame or embarrass the students publically. The girls were upset, and many tears ensued as they were suspended after a private session with each of their parents. The goal was to make this a learning experience they would never forget.

Humiliating a student can have the opposite of the intended effect. Students can shut down in defense, become resentful, and want to lash out. Or, instead of coming to view themselves as a responsible people, they may feel self-loathing. Young people need to be held accountable, think of the cause of their behavior, and not blame it on others. Talking it through and asking them to write about what they did and what they learned helps them develop self-reflection skills and allows them to take responsibility and maintain dignity.

Use Intrinsic, Not Extrinsic, Motivators

Becki shared,

When I first started teaching, I thought I needed to constantly control student behavior. I began by giving out hundreds of points, M&Ms, and all kinds of incentives. The class seemed to always get to the right amount of points for a class party around Halloween, Thanksgiving, or Valentine's Day, but I wanted them to behave well because it made the classroom a better place, not just because they wanted to have a party. I wanted the students to behave well because of an intrinsic sense of "doing the right thing." I gradually decreased the incentives and found their behavior was still good. Eventually I found that they needed no extrinsic rewards at all.

Over time, I found student behavior had a different quality when my expectations were specific, but my approach was less controlling. Their behavior improved dramatically. I told them that I trusted they would know how to control themselves, so I allowed them to talk and move around while they were working. We talked about what kind of talking and movement was appropriate in class. They suggested that the conversation needed to be about the work and the appropriate movement would be to "get something to complete the work."

A stimulating environment with less pressure from grades or rewards feels better to children. They become more engaged and intrinsically motivated, and their performance improves without the need of extrinsic rewards (Deci & Ryan, 1985).

**PUTTING TEACHER
SKILL INTO PRACTICE**

1. Keep a log of the students you remove from your room and the infraction that caused them to be removed. Are the students of all backgrounds removed in proportion to their presence in your classroom? How did the removal affect behavioral changes? What are some alternatives you could try instead of removing the student?

2. Think of two students with different kinds of repeated misbehavior. Think about the following questions:
   - What is causing the behavior?

     ○ Did the child know he or she was breaking a rule?

     ○ If the behavior problem was based on a lack of information, how can you remind the student of class procedures or rules?

     ○ If the student is lacking in social skills, how can you teach that skill (e.g., how to speak politely and not be demanding, or how to take turns)?

○ If the cause is attention seeking, how can you work with the student to find more appropriate ways to get your attention?

○ If the cause is a lack of impulse control, how can you work with the student on mechanisms to control behavior or to stop the student from being carried away?

• If the behavior is frequently disruptive or rebellious, you can ask yourself another set of questions.
  ○ What is your relationship with the student?

  ○ Does the child feel like a valued member of the classroom community, or does the child feel isolated from the others?

  ○ Is the child experiencing frustration from failure and lack of competence?

  ○ Does the child have enough autonomy?

Emotional and Physical Comfort **13**

WHY EMOTIONAL AND PHYSICAL COMFORT?

Teachers who have had the privilege of visiting other classrooms know that you can instantly get a sense of either wanting to be in that classroom or hoping for time to pass quickly so that you may leave. We believe that the attempt by teachers to create a classroom that is comfortable, both emotionally and physically, shapes whether you feel comfortable or not in the classroom. We learned from our SISP study that there are a number of things that teachers can do to help create that sense of comfort and well-being.

Here are the cues that you can use to determine whether or not the classroom is a comfortable place to work. Listen to the tone of the teacher's voice and the other voices in the classroom. Imagine you are a student in that class. Is the tone inviting and welcoming? What is the tone when students are speaking to one another? Is the pace just quick enough to pique your curiosity, but not so fast that you are getting lost and are unable to keep up? Is it unhurried enough that you can ask for help, but not too slow, so that your mind drifts off to other things? Are English learners being considered? Are the lessons understandable? Is the mood light-hearted? Is there a sense of fun and occasional laughter? All these aspects contribute to the feeling of emotional comfort for students in class.

The physical environment contributes to this sense, too. Students, like adults, respond to ambiance. In a classroom, the ambiance reflects a teacher's style and values, and teachers can enhance it by arranging the room to facilitate interaction and physical comfort. Look around your room. Is it relaxed, yet organized? Are norms and expectations posted? What are the messages on the walls? Is every student's culture and language represented somewhere in the room in artifacts, pictures, and words? Is achievement emphasized? Is each student's work displayed? Where does creativity fit into this classroom? All these aspects are evident the minute anyone walks into the room. In identity safe classrooms, the teacher makes the room physically and emotionally comfortable and as stress-free as possible.

EMOTIONAL AND PHYSICAL COMFORT: HOW TO DO IT

The Teacher's Attitude Sets the Stage

Our views of children dictate how we treat them. If we see them as manipulative, lazy, or selfish, it is not surprising that a quick response will be threatening or punitive. With a new puppy, we forgive the occasional accident on the rug as part of the learning process. Do we forgive our students when they "forget"? Sometimes we need to separate ourselves from the daily life to remind ourselves that we are here to help the students learn self-control and become responsible for their own learning. The ones with the least self-control are the ones who need us the most. By reflecting on our own attitudes, we can open ourselves to the students who irritate us. Sometimes teachers resent the students who take time away from the entire class. When the teacher shows empathy and patience as the student learns to change unwanted behaviors, the other students also learn how to be more accepting. The whole class wins as the community works together to bring each member into the fold.

We convey our attitude by both subtle and overt cues at any given moment and over time. What assumptions do we have about our students' intentions, abilities, and potential? Our rapport with the students, our body language, tone of voice, even the embedded presuppositions in the phrasing of our communication let them know how we feel about them personally, how we see the other students, and how we view the class as a whole.

Researchers have coined the term *microaggressions* for unintentional slights and derogatory remarks and insults aimed at persons of color that are at times so subtle that the perpetrator is not aware she is communicating them (Sue et al., 2007). These microaggressions include not only subtle attacks but also instances where a person's ideas are invalidated or the person is ignored altogether. The speaker might consider an interaction innocuous, but the target person could feel a host of negative feelings: attacked, invalidated, ignored, and/or disempowered.

Teachers can become aware of the harm of microaggressions and become more cognizant of their own behaviors and interactions among the students. While many behaviors are unconscious, a teacher's concerted effort to develop an understanding of the harm of seemingly small insults and offending comments that can be aimed at anyone considered "different" is an important part of creating an identity safe environment.

Provide a Personal Physical Place for Each Student

The premise of an identity safe learning environment is that students are naturally motivated to learn and treat each other well when they are cared for, nurtured, and challenged. The teacher sees himself as the architect of a positive classroom environment in both an emotional and a physical sense. Ken (Grade 4) described his view: "Belonging begins with a place. Students need to have a place that they call their own, a desk with their name on it, a group that includes them, and a teacher that respects them."

He took pride in all the small things that come together to make his classroom welcoming. He took photos of the students in different activities and put their pictures up around the room. Students could read in a cozy spot with a rug and pillows in the class library. He taught his students to arrange their binders and desks to be neat and well organized. He wanted them to learn and appreciate these important life and study skills. Ken gave extra guidance to anyone who had trouble with the process of organizing his or her workspace and materials.

Meera organized the environment in ways that naturally led to positive behavior. She arranged her fifth grade room to provide ample space for students to walk to the pencil sharpener or the door, leaving plenty of room for her to circulate. She made sure students were not so close that they distracted each other. During independent work time, she separated noisy activities from quiet ones.

In an identity safe classroom, all aspects of the environment, materials, room arrangement, seating plans, and walls are used to give particular messages that promote identity safety. Meera taught her students to change the classroom arrangement efficiently. They actually timed themselves to see how quickly and quietly they could move the furniture around. That allowed her to easily shift the class from group learning, to partners, to a circle for whole group activities.

"I See Myself Reflected on the Walls"

Karen loved setting up her fifth grade classroom as a "belonging" place. On one bulletin board, each student had a spot to post writing. Monthly, every child would select a finished piece of writing and place it on top of the previous one. By reading from the bottom, it was easy to see how that student progressed through the year. Some teachers worry about putting up less-than-perfect student work. This can be resolved by putting up a sign saying "Work in Progress." It is important that all students see their work displayed so that all students recognize that work improves with effort.

Ann's classroom was full of puppets and artifacts from the many countries represented by her second grade students. Quotes were up on the walls in all their different languages. Becki (Grade 1) published individual books and placed her students' photos on a page that said, "Meet the author." David's (Grade 5) classroom had a hanging timeline of US history. Every time they studied a historical event, a photo, report, or drawing was hung on the timeline. Over the year, he also added newspaper articles with current events and photos of class and school events. This gave his students a sense of connection and place for their lives as part of history.

The walls are also a great place to promote a college-going mentality. Becki reported,

> In my school, each classroom adopted a college. The teachers often selected their own college or university. They put up banners and pictures of the college and sometimes even tee shirts or the words to the school song. It gave a clear message that going to college was important and being prepared was our goal. We also had achievement walls with graphs to highlight class progress toward Common Core State Standards. Of course, we never highlighted individual student progress, which would create competition and embarrass students.

Julia's walls told the story of the many cultures that made up her fourth grade class with lots of photos of the students that she had taken across the year as well as posters of and motivating quotes from important leaders, writers, and inventors from all ethnic groups. If students do not see "others like me" reflected in the literature, curriculum, and on the walls, they are likely to feel invisible and get a sense that, "I don't belong here." In an identity safe classroom, the walls are a mirror in which all students can see themselves, what is valued, and what has been learned.

Equal, but Different

Perceived status differences undermine a student's capacity to have positive relationships and to feel safe and included. Inevitably, students enter with status differences, but these differences are either enhanced or diminished by teacher and student attitudes. For example, Nicole, one of Karen's fifth graders, had just transferred from a private school. She told

Karen that she left that school because, as a scholarship kid, she felt she was treated differently than the rest. Karen invited such discussions with her students and talked about both equity and diversity with them.

Karen recognized the importance of equalizing status and shared ways she worked to create it in her classroom. She taught the concept of *equal, but different* in a simple activity that demonstrated how everyone sees the world differently:

> I told my students, "We're going to create a creature. I'd like you to draw a large round yellow stomach. The creature has five purple hairy legs. This creature has a triangular shaped green head and a very short neck." When we were done, everyone held their pictures in a circle, and I said "Now hold on a minute, I gave everyone the same directions! What's going on here?" Then we talk about interpretation, style, personality, and perspective. "You all heard the same directions, but nobody interpreted it the same way, and that's okay. That's why we're here. We're here to learn from each other, understand we're different, and celebrate it. Look at this amazing group of monsters!"

Karen called their monsters "equal, but different posters," and she displayed every student's poster on the wall. She periodically reminded students of this norm, which she described as one of the most important values of her class.

In a similar vein, Becki made equal, but different family posters celebrating her students' different family constellations. Some families were big and had many members; others had just a mom or grandma and the children; others were blended—mom, stepdad, brothers, and stepsisters. And, some had two moms or two dads.

Pay Attention to Student Status and Cliques

Even when teachers monitor their own behavior and language, student power dynamics can lead to exclusion or hurtful interactions that undermine efforts to create an identity safe environment. Examine the social relationships in your classroom. Which children are more socially influential? Which qualities are valued among the students? Who tends to be excluded? Identity safe teachers continually search for ways to equalize social and academic status, especially in classrooms with a range of socio-economic and academic levels. Students can also be excluded when they look different from the others because of gender stereotypes, or because they are overweight or have physical or mental disabilities.

Karen and Ann provided different activities to alter group dynamics, to draw out different skills, and to equalize status. Karen shifted the perceptions of social status among her students by pointing to strengths they may not have previously considered important. She validated one student for assuming highly independent responsibilities at home and another by highlighting her ability to quickly grasp directions. Without drawing attention to particular students, she let the class know that girls and boys did not need to be limited by gender stereotypes and could play whatever games they chose. She also told the class that LGBT (lesbian, gay, bisexual, and transgender) people were valued members of society who needed to be treated fairly and respectfully.

Ann used puppets to let her students explore social identities in new ways. She found when their puppets spoke, some students were more outgoing and confident, and new social interactions occurred.

Teachers in identity safe classrooms consciously interrupt social cliques that form in their classrooms. They mix groups in a variety of ways that allow unique strengths to emerge and new relationships to develop. When Karen discussed the meaning of "equal, but different," she was able to build an appreciation of differences that helped alter the typical formation of in-groups and out-groups in her classroom.

Teacher Fairness

Even very young students are highly attuned to fairness. Becki found her first graders spent a lot of time at class meetings discussing "What is fair?" She said,

> I realized that my students are watching to be sure that everything I do is fair. So, we talk about what might be a fair solution to a problem. We don't always see it the same way, but I usually defer to their sense of fairness. For them, that is the basis of their trust in me.

Lauren described a similar situation when her young students were determining classroom jobs. She had a classroom telephone that was too high for some students to reach, so she logically gave the job of answering the phone to those who were tall enough to reach it. Over time, students let her know they did not think the system was fair. So, she opened the problem up for the students to generate a solution, and they did. They decided to have two people do the job, one who could reach and another who could answer the phone, making it fair for all to get a chance. Lauren commented on how it is not always easy to build responsibility and create a classroom community, but it was definitely worth the effort (Watson, 2003, p. 99).

Expressing Feelings

Karen's students learned to express feelings and empathy for one another through *status of the class*, an activity that can be done in less than five minutes, as described below:

> All the kids make a set of index cards numbered 1 through 10. When I say, "Okay, status of the class," they all take the cards out, select one, and hold it in front of them. I ask, "Anyone want to share?"
>
> "Oh, I'm a 10 today because I learned how to use my new skateboard."
>
> "I'm a 2 because my turtle died."
>
> "I'm a . . ."
>
> So, it allows everybody to share in their own way. And kids will say "Can we do status of the class? I need everyone to know I'm feeling really down." It's turned out to be really powerful.
>
> And kids will come to my desk in the morning and say, "I know we're not going to do status of the class first thing; I just want you to know that I'm really nervous because I'm going to get my braces on." They come and talk to me now, openly. Once I noticed that Veronica was only showing 2s and 3s but would never share her feelings with the class. So, I spoke to her privately, and she let out a rush of emotion, sharing some problems she had at home. That led to a parent conference, and now she is a much healthier kid.

Karen used this activity for a variety of purposes. It enabled students to identify and reflect on feelings and safely express them. It enabled Karen to quickly take stock of how her students were feeling and to identify any students who felt uncomfortable. Importantly, this activity allowed her to communicate to the students that how they felt mattered to her. It also permitted her to model empathy for them, so they could become more empathetic with one another.

Self-Affirmation as Protection Against Stereotype Threat

Throughout the book we describe ways to avoid situations and relationships that could create a sense of stereotype threat in students. We show, instead, ways that teachers can create a sense of true inclusion and belonging among all the students. This approach focuses on making sure that all the cues in the classroom say to every student, "You are welcomed here and valued as a student." This sense of being included and valued—of being identity safe—affirms that who students are and what they know and can do is important. A group of social psychological researchers demonstrated the power of what they call *self-affirmation* in making students feel a sense of identity safety at school (Cohen, Garcia, Apfel, & Master, 2006).

The researchers hypothesized that if students thought about what gives their lives meaning, it would confirm the students' sense of who they are. The reaffirmation of their personal values would serve as a buttress against stereotype threat. The notion of self-affirmation envisioned by these researchers is different from the popularized concept of affirmations that consists of listing qualities or attributes one might *want* to have. Instead, these affirmations refer to existing values and experiences that already make up a person's identity such as, "I am a religious person," or "My family means a lot to me," or "I try hard to do well with my school work."

The self-affirmation intervention conducted by Cohen et al. (2006) consisted of a brief in-class writing activity for middle school students at the beginning of the school year. In the assignment, African American and white seventh grade students were randomly assigned to one of two groups, the treatment group (the affirmation group) and the control group. Both groups were given a list of values. The affirmation group was told to select the two or three values *most important* to them personally and to write a paragraph about why these values were important to them.

The control group was asked to select the two or three values that were *least important* to them and to write a paragraph about why these values might be important to someone else (since the values were not important to them). Classroom teachers were unaware of the purpose or content of the research and were not told which students were in each group.

The results of this affirmation intervention are more powerful than one could expect. In the next fall term, the gap in grades between white students and African American students in the affirmation group was 40% lower than the gap in grades between white students and African American students in the control group who did not write about their important values. Claude Steele reports the results this way: "The grades of the no-affirmation control students kept going down, making the racial achievement gap in these classrooms even wider over the school term. What the affirmation did for the African American students . . . was to stop or slow this decline [in grades]" (2010, p. 175). This process led to a higher grade point average the next fall for those African American students in the affirmation group than those in the control group. That fall, the grades of the African American students in the affirmation group increased so that the percentage of those students who received a D or below in the course fell from 20% to 9%. Importantly, the white students' grades were, on average, the same in both the control and affirmation groups, perhaps because their sense of belonging was already established so they did not need additional affirmation.

This self-affirmation works this way: This elaborated image of one's self affirms a deep sense of who you are by reminding you of the resources you have to cope with the effects of stereotypes you may encounter (Sherman & Cohen, 2006; Steele, C. M., 1988).

These results offer exciting possibilities for educators in their efforts to alleviate stereotype threat. We explained this self-affirmation research in detail, because it has powerful potential and is at once simple and profound. If this small intervention had such dramatic results, what possibilities exist for an ongoing, consistent validation of students' sense of identity? It means that if teachers can find a way for students to feel connected with their personal sense of self as part of the daily experience of belonging and learning in the classroom, they can provide a natural buffer to stereotype threat.

Positive Presuppositions: Our Words Can Counter Stereotype Threat

A presupposition is an assumption that is hidden in the phrases we use to speak to one another (Costa, 2008). For example, in the phrase "Even Pablo will understand this lesson," the word *even* implies that Pablo is not smart and the lesson is easy. While the words don't directly state that this message will settle into Pablo's mind, these negative messages will accumulate over the course of many school years, and Pablo will form a view of himself as not too bright. Negative attitudes about school and disruptive behaviors are sure to result in the process.

For example, Dorothy tells about one middle school library she visited in which the only posted sign was, "Chew gum, get detention." There were no signs labeling the sections of the library, promoting specific books, or providing direction for use of the computers. There was nothing that would invite students to use the library to satisfy their own curiosity or interest. The message of this one sign is, "You are likely to misbehave and we won't have it."

Becki tells how she once saw a sign above the clock in a special education classroom saying, "Time passes, will you?" The teacher put up the poster to motivate students to use time wisely, but the underlying message was "You may not pass this class."

A number of upper grade students told Becki they frequently heard their parents warn, "I don't want you to turn into a statistic." Drumming this idea into students' minds feeds stereotype threat and the fear of failing, or worse yet, becoming a statistic by ending up in prison or dead. This may be a very real fear, but together with the many references to an achievement gap between white and other students, it can create a negative assumption about their ability into students' minds. As part of the self-reflection process, teachers not only can become cognizant of their words but also can learn to craft the opposite, positive presuppositions. These are assumptions, built into phrasing, that a student can and will be successful. When Becki first learned about stereotype threat, the use of positive presuppositions seemed like one of the most direct and powerful shifts she could make to counteract student fears of confirming a negative stereotype.

Here are a few examples of ways to say the same thing, using a negative presupposition on the left and incorporating a positive presupposition on the right:

Negative Presupposition	Positive Presupposition
Why do you always come to class unprepared?	When do you prepare for school, the night before or in the morning?
You only have half the answers right.	You clearly understood the concept of . . .

Language is powerful and gives subtle but consistent messages to students about your belief in their abilities. With awareness, you can monitor what comes out of your mouth, and with practice, you can shift the way you communicate your confidence in your students' potential to succeed.

Humor, a Two-Edged Sword

Humor can create an environment of emotional comfort or have the exact opposite effect. Ken described his goal of making his room "a very relaxed environment, where people can have fun. They can enjoy themselves. If you made a mistake, it's okay to laugh at yourself. It's all right." He achieved this goal through modeling and by teaching the norms of appropriate and respectful use of humor.

Sometimes humor, though well-intended, can backfire. Dorothy worked with one teacher who learned from a class meeting that her student, whose last name rhymed with spaghetti, did not like his teacher to call him "Fraghetti Spaghetti." What she thought of as an endearing name for this student made him feel self-conscious instead of loved. This teacher took the student's feelings seriously, apologized in front of the whole class, and vowed to call him by his first name only. This act of caring was a great model for this class of young students who were practicing forgiveness.

Time for Slowing the Pace

Karen shared, "Each day for 10 minutes after lunch, we do the 3 Rs: read, relax, reflect. I play music the kids bring to school, and they relax." Ann used her puppet collection for the same purpose. Each day, her second grade students chose a puppet to have on their desk for that day. She allowed five minutes for the children to have the puppets talk to their neighbors. This was a good opportunity for her many English learners to safely practice their oral language skills, and it contributed to a comfortable environment that did not feel hurried.

Like grown-ups, students need encouragement to get through long weeks of work. Karen described the little "Friday dance" she does with her students to brighten their spirits at the end of the week:

> Only on Fridays, first thing in the morning, then right after recess and right after lunch, they start the little dance as they walk in the door. As we dance, we talk about what we're looking forward to on the weekend, such as "I get to sleep in, play my games, eat my waffles, get to read books on my bed." By the time they get in the door, they're all sitting down, because they're thinking about what they get to do tomorrow morning!

Supportive Learning Strategies

Students react to the emotional climate of a classroom. So, strategies that take them into consideration lead to more comfort, more learning, and more retention of what has been learned. When learning is scaffolded, students do not see tasks as an insurmountable mountain, but a series of manageable steps. Finding the correct level of difficulty for students, neither too hard nor too easy, maximizes their motivation. Using materials that appeal to visual, auditory, and kinesthetic ways of learning lets students choose a comfortable way to approach the content.

Finding ways to engage students' hearts and minds together enhances the possibility of keeping them focused and feeling comfortable. Meaningful and relevant topics turn writing from a chore into a way to express feelings and ideas. Using curricular content to solve real-life problems in the school also captivates students. For example, they get excited if they learn about computation while measuring wood to make a stage for a puppet show.

Peer teaching capitalizes on the social nature of learning and makes new content meaningful and fun. One way to implement peer teaching is to divide students into two groups. Each group reads a different portion of the book and has to teach it to the others. Another way is to have students read a passage and then explain it without looking at the book, while the partner checks the book to see if the explanation is correct.

CHALLENGES AND DILEMMAS

The main challenge for teachers in creating emotional and physical comfort is finding ways to address the wide range of differing and sometimes contradictory needs in a class of students. We will look at two of the dilemmas:

1. what to do when differing socioeconomic income levels get in the way, and

2. accommodating the differing needs of special-needs students.

These are among the many challenges identity safe teachers face when providing emotional and physical comfort for the range of students in every classroom.

When Some Students Have More Than Others

A dilemma is created when some students have more access to fancier clothes, special toys, and better opportunities than others. Clearly students are aware of socioeconomic differences, but the teacher needs to do her best to level the playing field by not asking questions or having activities that exacerbate the differences. Meera noticed who had more opportunities when students shared about their vacations at circle time. To avoid the problem, she selected a topic for sharing, making sure it was one all students could relate to, such as having everyone describe a favorite pet, or how to get along with siblings, or their favorite music, or something they hoped to learn that year.

How to Balance the Needs of Special-Needs Students With the Needs of the Rest of the Class

Students with special needs can feel unique stresses in the daily life of a classroom. Praising effort and avoiding comparisons between students will increase emotional comfort for students whose accumulation of failure has made them ultrasensitive. In one incident, a parent complained to Becki about one of the well-loved teachers:

> The parents reported that their son was traumatized by two of the teacher's practices. He hated the color card chart for discipline posted on the wall in full view. Everyone started the day with a green card, and after an infraction, a yellow card replaced the green card. For repeated infractions, the yellow card was replaced by the red card.
>
> I knew that many teachers like the card system, saying it allows for immediate communication and provides a reminder for students without taking class time to verbally call attention to behavior issues. In this case, the card mortified this young fellow. According to his parents, he actually had nightmares about it, because he never ended the day with a green card.
>
> The other practice was her lunch reward system. If students had a week of good behavior, they could join their teacher for a special lunch. This fellow could never string together enough good days to win this reward. When I discussed this with the teacher, she explained that she treated all her students the same. I pointed out that perhaps other students were a bit bothered or possibly might have also felt stress from these two systems, but kept it to themselves. Yet, for this boy, these two practices led to an extreme sense of discomfort. The teacher, who was a reflective person, saw this as an eye-opener. She was able to find alternate ways to ensure this boy and the other students would not feel humiliation or become frustrated by impossible-to-reach rewards.

Students with special needs have varied prerequisites for feeling comfortable in a classroom. Some autistic students prefer blank walls free of distractions. This need conflicts with the needs of the other students, who respond to bright walls filled with pictures and student work. There is no single answer for handling such a dilemma. The teacher may need to experiment with different sections of the room and then note everyone's reactions to decide how to adorn the walls.

The identity safe teacher intentionally sets up her classroom to accommodate as many needs as possible. She also discusses these issues with the class, having them help generate solutions. She can say, "I know some of you need absolute silence to concentrate, while others like music with a beat to help you stay focused. What are some ideas on how to handle this?" In this way, empathy is built along with an appreciation of our differing tastes, needs, and learning styles.

PUTTING EMOTIONAL AND PHYSICAL COMFORT INTO PRACTICE

Plan Your Walls to Include All Students

Idea	What do you have?	What do you need?
Norms, standards, and expectations		
Student writing		
Photos of students		
Photos of role models from all cultures and ethnicities represented among students		
Student art		
Content review		
College-going motivation		

Use Positive Presuppositions: Change the Negative Phrases Into Positive Presuppositions

Negative Presupposition	Positive Presupposition
It is not realistic to think you can go from being a C student to the honor roll in one quarter.	It is great you have made it your goal to get on the honor roll. I know you can do it by working every day with a steady focus.
You better study for the test, or you will fail.	
Since you don't know English, here is a picture dictionary with an easier assignment.	
You will never be ready for college if you don't turn in your homework.	
Here is an easier book, so you can understand the words.	
How can you find anything in that desk?	
When will you learn to sit still?	

This tool is also available for download at **www.corwin.com/identitysafe.**

Attention to Prosocial Development

14

WHY ATTENTION TO PROSOCIAL DEVELOPMENT?

In this book, we refer to the social nature of learning many times as we describe the practice of creating an identity safe classroom. Explicitly, we recognize that the process of teaching and learning is based on a fundamental human transaction between the teacher and her students and among the students with one another. Learning is not an input/output process, but a complex social and intellectual process that occurs most successfully when teachers know their students and have a trusting relationship with them.

Throughout the book we focus on many ways for teachers to think about the classroom from the students' perspectives and to incorporate their ideas, experiences, and skills into the process of teaching. The purpose of this chapter is to dig a bit deeper into the ways that teachers can help students develop the behaviors and habits that create a classroom in which most interactions are positive, caring, and conducive to learning. Teachers can help students develop these behaviors and habits through providing them with social skills lessons, academic activities that require social interactions, and class meetings. We believe these efforts will help (1) prepare students for a life of successful social interactions in school, work, and their personal lives; (2) create a positive classroom environment that is conducive to learning; and (3) promote academic achievement, when combined with activities that develop oral language, writing, and reading skills.

At each developmental level, students need guidance and practice in behaving in prosocial ways. Teachers can facilitate this learning by giving students opportunities for nonacademic discussions, such as class meetings about how to settle disputes on the play yard or how to allocate time at the computers in the classroom. In addition, teachers who help students interpret disagreements and find solutions to arguments, rather than acting as judge and jury, will help students grow into mature social beings. And, through academic lessons and activities that promote cooperation and mutual respect, students will gain more mature understanding of other students and other backgrounds.

The inclusion of prosocial learning helps students participate in building a community of learners in which the highest level of learning is made more possible for each student. Students can learn how to analyze situations and alter their behavior to fit different cultural or social situations. Additionally, when students know that problems will be handled, they are freed from worrying about conflicts and can focus on learning. Since the basic need for belonging causes children to want to fit into a classroom, when they have prosocial skills and feel included, they are more engaged in the curriculum and life in the classroom.

ATTENTION TO PROSOCIAL DEVELOPMENT: HOW TO DO IT

Class Meetings

Class meetings offer a multifaceted opportunity for teaching prosocial values, including sharing, appreciating, showing empathy, and solving problems. The temptation to skip meetings when pressed for time may actually cost more in time spent resolving conflicts and solving interpersonal problems. Karen (Grade 5) explained that an important quality of class meetings is that differences are recognized and dealt with, rather than diminished or ignored. These nonevaluative interactions helped Karen and students to get to know each other better. She explained,

> That means it's a safe place for you to be yourself, where you can
> be honest and open, have differences in opinion, and learn how
> to accept each other and agree to disagree or to share something.
> And with all the kids knowing that, it's amazing what comes out.

Karen made simple statements modeling empathy for her students, such as, "I think that having your turtle die must have made you feel very sad." And she asked questions such as, "How did you feel when that happened?" With strict rules against put-downs and belittling others, she ensured no one was teased or made fun of and that humor was not hurtful. Her students regularly shared and practiced responding without being judgmental:

> I tell them, "What happens stays in that circle; scream and yell and feel." We've gotten to the point now where kids can say, "I need to have a class meeting, because I had an incident." The kids are just really comfortable being able to say how they feel in the room.

Melania described how she uses class meeting to teach particular social skills needed by her fourth grade class:

> All prosocial skills can be taught through a simple process: explaining the purpose of the skill, modeling it, role-playing how it is done, and then practicing. I made sure to highlight it when I saw a skill we had discussed being used.

Her observations show authentic appreciation for students' behaviors and remind other students of the prosocial behaviors she is teaching. There are a variety of models with specific steps for how to set up class meetings, such as Developmental Studies Center's *Ways We Want Our Class to Be* (1996).

Teachers who want to help students become socially aware and gain skills in prosocial behavior can do so by helping them to see that behaviors have different meanings in different cultures and different families. For example, Becki said,

> I became aware that interrupting, which was no big deal in my family, was seen as extremely rude in some cultures. I eventually decided not only to work on not interrupting, but, as a principal, to use our weekly assembly to teach the whole school how to interrupt, when necessary, respectfully. I asked three students to role-play walking up to two others in conversation, pausing, saying, "May I interrupt?" and then waiting for a response. The teachers followed the lesson with practice sessions during their class meetings. It was a pleasure to see students remembering and practicing it when they came up to me in the schoolyard.

Social understanding includes empathy to sense the emotional signals given off by others and the capacity to tune in to their verbal and nonverbal messages. It also encompasses awareness of how the social world operates. This becomes even more complex in a diverse social milieu, where the signals have cultural nuances. For example, in Asian cultures, not looking into someone's eyes is a sign of respect, while in the mainstream American culture, looking away is a signal that someone is not paying attention. Teachers can explain the importance of this kind of awareness and discuss social cognition with the students. Without stereotyping, they can have the students, themselves, identify their own styles of communication and celebrate the rich differences in the classroom. They also can also talk about how to read all types of emotional cues and about ways to respond to them as part of giving Attention to Prosocial Development.

Teach Empathy, Mutual Respect, and Intergroup Understanding

Deep and ongoing self-reflection is part of the cycle of inquiry for teachers working to create identity safe classrooms. When teachers reflect on themselves and define what empathy, respect, and intergroup understanding mean to them, they can find ways to define, model, and teach behaviors that reflect these values. Mindful teachers look beyond what would have made them feel safe when they were students. Instead, they consider the perspectives of each of their students, recognizing the students come from different backgrounds.

Becki described an example of a teacher's unintentional miscue for some of her students:

> I once observed a kindergarten teacher dismissing children by asking them to share what they ate for breakfast, saying, "All the students who ate eggs for breakfast can go to recess." A big group left the circle. Then she said, "Now all of you who had cereal for breakfast can go," and another big group left. Little by little students were dismissed, leaving about three students in the circle. "What did you have?" she asked each of them. Two had rice, and a third had no breakfast. I watched as those three seemed to slink away from the circle.

The kindergarten teacher did not anticipate that her question might make any child feel different and self-conscious. Teachers should not be paralyzed by such unintended negative responses. When something like this happens, teachers can repair any slights by directly addressing the impacted students, saying they hadn't thought about other foods for breakfast and were so glad their students had shared. They might find a book such as *How My Parents Learned to Eat*, by I. R. Friedman (1984), or pictures or other representations of different meals to share with the class at another point in the near future. What may have been a self-conscious moment can turn into a teachable moment where these children are the teachers!

By contrast, the needs of the child who did not have breakfast are concrete and very important. Teachers must connect with the child and express a willingness to help address this problem. Hopefully, teachers have some resources available to give hungry children access to nutritious food.

To set the standard for mutual respect and intergroup understanding, a teacher can give living examples of how empathy involves being able to see the world from someone else's point of view and feeling compassion for that person. One popular model of teaching empathy involves bringing a young infant to a classroom on a monthly basis over a year. Students observe and ask questions, learning about how the baby grows and what it takes to care for her. Researchers found that at any grade level, the experience helps students feel empathy and gain insight into themselves and others (Gordon, 2005). Similarly, caring for plants, animals, or even bugs can enhance students' feelings of empathy and teach them about how the world works and what we can do, as people, to care for it.

Everyday experiences can provide the most important opportunities for students to learn empathy and understanding. When a student is frustrated or sad or needing help, the teacher can support efforts by other students to help the one who needs it. The idea that teachers and students "leave themselves at the doorstep" is both psychologically unsound and impossible to do. Teachers who make space for empathetic behavior will go a long way in teaching students that who they are and what they experience matters and can be accepted in the classroom.

Students can gain intergroup understanding from experiences with their classmates and from conversations with their teachers, too. Students love to hear stories from their teacher's life. In one example, Meera shared her Indian culture with her fifth grade students:

> Students feel connected when they know their teacher. I am not this mystery person, but a mom who once had children their age. I found out that sharing about my culture gives students from different ethnic and cultural backgrounds confidence to share about themselves. Students are not shy to say they like certain music or food. We talk about the different festivals and holidays, we talk about the food and clothes. Circle time becomes our place to share culture. It is amazing to see how my students are in awe when they find out about certain special things about a culture.

Through role-plays, literature analysis, and writing followed by discussion, these values come alive as part of daily life in the classroom. And when conflicts do arise, these experiences can help student deconstruct and analyze problems to find solutions in the spirit of these values.

Respecting Different Points of View

We have been talking a lot about learning about different points of view. The next step in becoming an empathetic, respectful student is learning to work within these differences in a positive, productive manner. Consensus-building skills can help students learn to listen to others, keep an open mind, and resolve problems in ways that are agreeable to all. Tools for consensus building can especially help children who tend to be argumentative in academic or social situations (Taccogna & Bonstingl, 2003). Students can learn consensus-building phrases such as, "so you're saying," or "would you consider?" or "can you help me understand?"

Integrating Prosocial Teaching Into the Academic Curriculum

Prosocial teaching and academic instruction integrate naturally. Prosocial teaching is engaging and draws students into a content area. Students get excited taking on a controversial topic to solve a real-world problem. The air becomes electric when they read about an issue, define and write their positions, and translate their ideas into a debate. They are practicing mutual respect as they listen to each other's points of view. Some lessons may not have prosocial content but require collaboration. In a cooperative science lesson on magnetism, how the students work together will determine how they arrive at their conclusions. An identity safe teacher highlights that working together is an extremely important social skill for many things in life. Everything from mapping the genome to producing a Hollywood film is a collaborative effort. We will examine a few ways to seamlessly integrate prosocial teaching in all content areas without taking time away from academics.

Oral Language, Reading, and Writing

Literature, writing, and discussion are rich sources for gaining empathy and learning about other cultures. Students can role-play or write from another person's perspective. Good literature, with rich examples of emotional and social interactions that lead to higher-level thinking, can be found at every grade level. Consideration of a character's motives, choices, and situations is ripe with prosocial lessons. Students can analyze the different problems faced by the characters by considering the multiple points of view and moral dilemmas.

Becki shared,

> I developed my own curriculum for first graders. Students dictated
> class stories for invented animal characters. We incorporated the

values of friendship, freedom, respect, and diversity. Then the students discussed the ideas and wrote their own stories. Finally, we took the stories and made class books, reader's theatre, and puppet shows they presented to the class. The students loved it.

When I taught fourth grade, the students worked with the same animal characters and wrote chapters to share with kindergarten buddies. They illustrated the stories and made up skits for their kindergarten friends. My classroom was charged with excitement during these creative efforts. Not only did their collaboration improve, their grades did too.

Meera's fifth grade class examined feelings about racism in discussions of the book *The Great Gilly Hopkins* (Patterson, 1978):

I think it is important to have these courageous conversations on race. They can use literature, like when Gilly didn't want to touch the hands of Mr. Randolph because he was African American. I ask the students why.

Karen also used *The Great Gilly Hopkins* to help her fifth graders link to American history:

When we read about Gilly Hopkins, we discussed slavery. My students learned that the Chinese had been slaves, too. My Chinese students didn't like it. I asked them, "What are you feeling, did you know that?" So we discussed how slavery has been going on since the beginning of time. . . . Whoever has the power wants to dominate others to make themselves feel better, and then take their rights away.

The book *The Great Gilly Hopkins* is not for teachers who are faint of heart. Becki shared,

Once I had complaint from a substitute who felt Gilly's strong language was not appropriate. She was uncomfortable with Gilly's internal racist monologue. Both Karen and Meera saw it as a chance to discuss issues of race. As the students progressed through the book, they noticed Gilly's racist attitudes transformed as her relationship with Mr. Randolph grew. They noted that Gilly also became a more compassionate person.

Literature gives countless opportunities for class discussions that go into complex and deep prosocial issues.

History and Social Studies

History is also full of social lessons. Becki shared,

My fifth grade students studied US history, and they dressed up as characters from history, writing and delivering speeches from their characters' points of view. When studying the Lewis and Clark expedition, I asked my students to imagine how Sacagawea felt. They wrote about the expedition from her perspective. This writing assignment showed the students the powerful difference in perspectives in history written by those who inhabited the land versus history written by those who explored "new" lands.

A storyteller also came to our class to share stories of courage and resilience. Her family stories brought the civil rights era to life. She also shared amazing tales of African Americans during the gold rush.

Inviting artists, storytellers, and poets from the various backgrounds of the students into the classroom provides students with historical contexts woven with rich intercultural experiences in the arts, all of which help to enhance prosocial development.

Meera asked her class to think about who wrote their history books. She augmented textbooks with primary source materials she found on the Internet. She also used the primary sources to teach her fifth graders to critically analyze their textbooks.

The Arts

Art is a natural venue for emotional expression. Studying art forms offers rich opportunities for students to learn about the feelings of others and to express their own feelings and ideas. Arts education bridges cognitive and emotional development. The artistic expression and creativity found in every culture can be used to affirm student identities and to motivate and bolster academic achievement (Nieto, 1999).

Including music from many cultures and styles can promote a sense of belonging and expand their knowledge as students share music that is important to them. They may find that, though they share an interest in various types of popular American music, they can introduce other music to the class that may be "new" to other students. Meera shared how she uses music with her fifth grade class:

When we do our circle, I'll say, "What kind of music do we like?" One day the kids started naming American pop culture figures and musicians. So the kids are naming these bands; then, this Latina girl in my class said, "Oh, I like Green Day," and everybody shared, "Oh, that's good, you know."

It came to my turn, because they won't let me off the hook, so I had to share, too. I said, "I really like Indian music. I know you guys haven't heard it, but maybe one day I'll bring it to share. I love Indian music because I grew up with it, so I listen to it over here, and it's so nice." Then the Latina girl said, "You know, when my mom plays Mexican songs it makes me feel like we're back in Mexico." Until she heard me share about Indian music, she wanted to be like everybody else. So, the very next day she brought Mexican music.

One great benefit of arts education is that some students who have not done well academically do have strong skills in singing, acting in plays, playing instruments, dancing, or reciting their poems that allow them to shine and give them meaningful hooks into the business of being a student. The arts can be a bridge to positive feelings about school and renewed effort in other academic areas.

Room for Prosocial Teaching in Every Curricular Area

In science, dilemmas provide opportunities to use content that connects social and academic learning. Debates on health, technology, and environmental issues are rich with opportunities for students to examine multiple perspectives and ethical questions. Physical education and sports require team efforts. Problem solving in statistics, probability, logic, and mathematics can link academics to prosocial situations.

Parents as Partners for Prosocial Learning

All parents want their children to get along with others and feel emotionally safe. They know and love their children and have important information that can help teachers understand their children's culture and background. To bridge home and school cultures, invite parents into the classroom to bring in home traditions, language, and personal stories. Parents are an excellent resource, no matter how many cultures and ethnic groups are in a classroom. Whether parents bring in Ethiopian cuisine or Salvadoran *pupusas*, or simply participate in an interview about their childhood for a homework assignment, teachers gain insights into their students' family lives when parents participate. Subsequently, parents will come to feel safe themselves to bring up cultural issues or concerns that will help the teacher support their children better. Building a relationship with parents creates a partnership for supporting their children when problems arise.

Some parents do not appreciate the value of prosocial learning. Karen shared, "I actually had a parent one year who said, 'Could you quit with the fluff?'" After that, on back-to-school night, Karen made sure to give an overview of the purpose of her prosocial curriculum and how it linked to her rigorous academic program. At parent conferences, she ensured that parents understood how their children were doing not only with academics but also with learning prosocial skills.

Parents are most likely to be convinced when they witness improvement and see their children thriving academically and socially. If parents understand identity safety, they can strengthen identity safety for their children in their homes and social environments. They see that a focus on identity safety validates the child's culture, validates the family, and affirms each student's social identity.

CHALLENGES AND DILEMMAS

We will explore two challenges with Attention to Prosocial Development.

1. We will examine the challenge of different family/cultural values that may clash with those in the classroom. This is especially important when the teacher is from a different background than the students.

2. Then we will look at how to help students learn to adjust to behavioral expectations in different situations.

By observing how individual students respond to specific experiences in the classroom, teachers can be aware of when their students feel tensions that may be rooted in cultural understandings. Having the students share from their own lives acknowledges cultural differences and leaves room for variations among common practices of a particular community. Thereby, teachers do not make assumptions about children's behavior based on their ethnicities, and yet cultural factors that influence behavior and prosocial development are recognized and valued (Gutierrez & Rogoff, 2003).

Teachers who want to create an identity safe classroom are careful not to accept cultural explanations as excuses for accepting inappropriate behavior. Once, when Dorothy was visiting her son's high school in a high-achieving neighborhood, she noticed several African American students lingering outside the classroom doors well after the bell had rung for classes to begin. When she went to the principal to inquire about this, she was told that the teachers were trying to be kind to the students and not pressure them! This attitude is not an isolated one. Ladson-Billings (1994) describes a teacher who held her African American students to a lower standard than the white students, because she felt sorry for them and wanted to show them that she cared.

How do teachers help students come to a shared understanding of how to talk, work, write, dress, and relate to others while in school? Some students come to school with *cultural capital*, that is language, tastes, values, and behaviors that signify social prestige as defined by those in society with the greatest power (Bourdieu, 1986). For children who do not come from mainstream backgrounds, cultural capital can be acquired.

Teachers have the challenge of teaching mainstream expectations without demeaning a child's background or making value judgments about what is "right." Standard English, taught in school, is needed for formal speaking and writing. Teachers can explain the necessity for learning the standard way so that the many cultural and language groups in the United States can communicate. Meanwhile, teachers can give students opportunities to share home languages and dialects. Instead of saying, "That is the wrong way to say . . . ," they can say, "In standard English, it is said or written this way . . . ." Beginning at a very young age, students can learn this skill, sometimes called *code-switching*. Students code-switch all the time as they incorporate slang into their lexicons. This skill will help students function successfully in many situations. When explaining code-switching, teachers have a unique opportunity to communicate that what students bring to school has value and to appreciate their identities and home cultures while preparing them to be successful in the world.

PUTTING ATTENTION TO PROSOCIAL DEVELOPMENT INTO PRACTICE

How will you carve out the time? How will you integrate it into your curriculum?

Prosocial Skill Building	Making the Time	Integrating Into Your Lessons
Class meetings		
Prosocial reflection at the end of a lesson		
Empathy and respect		
Intergroup understanding		
Academic controversy		
Consensus building		
Integrating prosocial skills in curricular areas		
Involving the parents		

Part V Summary

A caring environment creates a sense of inclusion and belonging in students that permeates every experience in an identity safe classroom. Meera (Grade 5) describes,

> There is no specific curriculum. I use ideas from different people. We do a lot of interest surveys and a lot of getting-to-know-each-other activities. We set the norms as a class. We talk about rights and responsibilities; we all have a right to learn, and we all have a responsibility to ensure that everyone learns. We come up with things together, and we invest in that.

Teacher Skill in identity safety is the marriage of strong instructional strategies with management systems that address the academic *and* social needs of each student. Strong relationships are formed by including all students' ideas and experiences while promoting class unity founded on the principle of equal status. The teacher orchestrates a calm, well-managed, emotionally and physically comfortable space.

By focusing on Emotional and Physical Comfort, teachers can create a space for students to freely explore, try out new ideas and ways of interacting, and take risks. When a teacher creates a feeling of equal status, students from varied backgrounds and with different skill sets feel accepted. Students learn to express feelings and feel protected from social rejection, because they know conflicts will be addressed fairly. Positive presuppositions and affirmations of their distinct identities counter stereotypes from the greater society.

In an identity safe classroom, teachers give full Attention to Prosocial Development by explicitly teaching and giving students regular chances to practice caring behavior as part of the "way we do business" every day. The teacher is highly attuned to students' cultures, needs, and interactions. From that awareness, needed skills can be taught, problems can be addressed, and a strong empathetic community can be formed. In turn, a sense of belonging and academic and social competence comes from all teacher messages and student experiences in the classroom and at school.

Part V References

Bourdieu, P. (1986). The forms of capital. In J. G. Richardson (Ed.), *Handbook of theory and research for sociology in education* (pp. 241–248). New York, NY: Greenwood Press.

Braithwaite, V. (2000). Values and restorative justice in schools. In H. Strang & J. Braithwaite (Eds.), *Restorative justice: Philosophy to practice* (pp. 121–144). Aldershot, UK: Ashgate.

Cohen, G., Garcia, J., Apfel, N., & Master, A. (2006). Reducing the racial achievement gap: A social psychological intervention. *Science, 313*, 1307–1310.

Costa, A. (2008). *The school as a home for the mind: Creating mindful curriculum, instruction, and dialogue.* Thousand Oaks, CA: Corwin.

Deci, E., & Ryan, R. M. (1985). *Intrinsic motivation and self-determination in human behavior.* New York, NY: Plenum Press.

Development Studies Center. (1996). *Ways we want our class to be: Class meetings that build commitment to kindness and learning.* Oakland, CA: Author.

Friedman, I. R. (1984). *How my parents learned to eat.* New York, NY: Houghton Mifflin.

Gordon, M. (2005). *Roots of empathy.* Toronto, ON: Thomas Allen & Son.

Gutierrez, K., & Rogoff, B. (2003). Cultural ways of learning. *Educational Researcher 32*, 19–25.

Ladson-Billings, G. (1994). *Dreamkeepers.* San Francisco, CA: Jossey-Bass.

Nieto, S. (1999). *The light in their eyes: Creating multicultural learning communities.* New York, NY: Teachers College Press.

Patterson, K. (1978). *The great Gilly Hopkins.* New York, NY: HarperCollins.

Sherman, D. K., & Cohen, G. L. (2006). The psychology of self-defense: Self-affirmation theory. In M. P. Zanna (Ed.), *Advances in Experimental Social Psychology, 38*, 183–242. San Diego, CA: Academic Press.

Steele, C. M. (1988). The psychology of self-affirmation: Sustaining the integrity of the self. In L. Berkowitz (Ed.), *Advances in experimental social psychology* (pp. 261–302). New York, NY. Academic Press.

Steele, C. M. (2010). *Whistling Vivaldi and other clues to how stereotypes affect us.* New York, NY: W. W. Norton.

Steele, D. M. (2012). Identity-safe school environments, creating. In J. A. Banks (Ed.), *Encyclopedia of diversity in education* (Vol. 1, pp. 1125–1128). Thousand Oaks, CA: Sage.

Sue, D. W., Capodilupo, C. M., Torino, G. C., Bucceri, J. M., Holder, A. M. B., Nadal, K. L., & Marta, E. (2007). Racial microaggressions in everyday life: Implications for clinical practice. *American Psychologist, 62*(4), 271–286.

Taccogna, J., & Bonstingl, J. J. (2003). *Powerful teaching: Developmental assets in curriculum and instruction.* Minneapolis, MN: Search Institute Press.

Watson, M. (2003). *Learning to trust: Transforming difficult elementary classrooms through developmental discipline.* San Francisco, CA: Jossey-Bass.

Wolfe, P. (1998). Revisiting effective teaching. *Educational Leadership, 56*(3), 61–64.

Epilogue

Where do you start? How can you begin to put the pieces of the identity safety puzzle together? What is the first thing to know in order to develop an identity safe classroom? The book describes 14 different, but related, factors that constitute identity safe teaching practices. We have tried to describe the whole and its many parts, and it is a lot to take in. But let us try to encourage you to start, and start simply, with a few important things in mind.

First, though we have showed it in many ways, we want to underline that students cannot become successful at learning without having a foundational sense of belonging. Often people talk about social and emotional learning as an add-on, but we cannot overstate the strength of the link between students' sense of belonging and their ability to focus on learning unencumbered by worries that their social identity will become a barrier to academic success. Having a sense of belonging is a condition for learning that must be met for all students, no matter what their background.

Because of this fundamental need, building positive relationships with each student and among the students is the first thing a teacher who wants to create an identity safe classroom must focus on. There are many ideas about how to do this in the book, but one can begin simply with a sincere and warm greeting to each student every morning. This greeting can be elaborated with a check-in via class meetings or with a "state of the class" activity as described by Karen in Part V, in which she asks students to indicate how they are feeling by giving a rating from one to ten with numbered cards. This process lets teachers "take the temperature" of the students and gives them the chance to follow up with students who are not having a good day. Showing the students you are glad they are there and you are interested in how things are going for them is a huge first step in building positive relationships.

Another step in creating a sense of identity safety among students is to listen to and learn from them. Encourage students to share their ideas, perspectives, and interests. Use this student knowledge-base by bringing their voices into the classroom with activities that include their families, skills, and energies. That includes using world languages, music, literature, representative people, and any other artifacts of students' lives and cultures every day in one way or another.

We propose many ideas about ways to use the students' ideas, interests, and languages as regular resources for teaching, because there is evidence that being colorblind actually makes classrooms less safe for students of color. This applies to other differences as well. Trying to be colorblind does not erase the differences that matter to students who have already felt the power of negative stereotypes. Classrooms can be places where differences are appreciated and included to enhance learning and belonging.

It may seem as if it takes too much time to help students learn to work together on an academic task, or to manage the use of computers in a productive, fair way, or to resolve a conflict. But the time it takes to help students work together may save time in having to correct difficult behavior again and again. Students can learn from one another and help one another only when they are taught prosocial skills and given many opportunities to practice—just as they learn math or how to read. Not only is the ability to work well with others useful throughout one's life in family relationships and in work, but also, importantly, the students have a lot to offer one another. Teaching them, starting in the beginning of the year, to be responsible; to feel ownership of the classroom space, materials, and procedures; and to be responsive to the needs of others will help to create a harmonious and productive classroom.

An essential ingredient of an identity safe classroom is a challenging, meaningful, and supported curriculum for every student. Providing a challenging curriculum for everyone can be one of the hardest aspects of teaching for an identity safe teacher. Being able to differentiate the curriculum for the wide range of social and academic skills students bring to school will take ongoing observation, thoughtful appraisal of students' levels of achievement, and creative solutions for managing the classroom. Use positive presuppositions to model your high expectations for the students. This approach will help your students meet the Common Core State Standards, because it will help them engage in higher order thinking and become more involved in directing their own learning. Work with other teachers to share ideas with the specific challenges you have, so you can work toward the first goal of teaching—to support the full development of each student.

Finally, continually look at your own practice, considering the classroom from the point of view of each student. Is it a positive, pleasant, and challenging place to work? Do all the students see themselves as valued members of the class with something important to offer? And, how do *you* feel? Are you able to seek help with any difficulties you have? Can you find at least one supportive colleague with whom you can share ideas and concerns? Reaching out to others can help you feel more included, supported, and identity safe, yourself.

One caution. As you consider your practice, try to confirm that you are being consistent in your efforts to build an identity safe classroom. That is, no matter how much you focus on bringing in the student voices, or providing a challenging curriculum, or including materials from many cultures, if certain children are given primarily remedial lessons or disciplined more frequently, or if they are "managed" instead of included, it will not be possible to create a really identity safe environment. Trust between the teacher and students is built on truly inviting each one into every aspect of the classroom, so they can develop to their full potential.

We believe that teachers who work to create identity safe classrooms will become more energized and motivated as they find their classrooms more exciting and successful in helping students learn. These teachers will feel connected to student learning and development in ways that are enriching and motivating, because it will keep them in touch with why they became teachers in the first place.

In the introduction we posited that *identity safe teaching practices* can serve as an antidote to stereotype threat by creating a sense of belonging and engagement for all students. Identity safe teaching practices are especially important for students whose social identities are too often associated with school failure. We believe, based on our research, that being in an identity safe classroom can help turn around cycles of repeated failure for many students. It will take a concerted effort to change the current trajectory of disproportionate academic and social failure of Latino and African American students. That responsibility belongs to the society as a whole, not only teachers and administrators. However, as educators, it is imperative we play a significant role in that process. We hope this book will provide an impetus for conversations among teachers and all who work in the field of education who want to make classrooms better places for all children by making them identity safe.

Index

CORWIN
A SAGE Company

The Corwin logo—a raven striding across an open book—represents the union of courage and learning. Corwin is committed to improving education for all learners by publishing books and other professional development resources for those serving the field of PreK–12 education. By providing practical, hands-on materials, Corwin continues to carry out the promise of its motto: **"Helping Educators Do Their Work Better."**